Astrology and Psychology

A Dialogue on the 21st Century

Mauro Silva

Copyright 2013 by Mauro Silva

No part of this book may be reproduced or transcribed in any form or by any means, electronic or mechanical, including photocopying or recording or by any information storage and retrieval system without written permission from the author and publisher, except in the case of brief quotations embodied in critical reviews and articles. Requests and inquiries may be mailed to: American Federation of Astrologers, Inc., 6535 S. Rural Road, Tempe, AZ 85283.

ISBN-10: 0-86690-647-9
ISBN-13: 978-0-86690-647-0

Translator: David Gilman
Cover Design: Jack Cipolla

Published by:
American Federation of Astrologers, Inc.
6535 S. Rural Road
Tempe, AZ 85283

Printed in the United States of America

Contents

Introduction	v
Chapter 1, Interpretation of the Birth Chart	1
Chapter 2, Trait Theories: Rescuing a Tradition	11
Chapter 3, Introduction to Minimalist Astrology	37
Chapter 4, Biological Foundations	63
Chapter 5, Michel Gauquelin's Research	83
Chapter 6, Skeptics and Pseudo-Skeptics	107
Chpater 7, Final Remarks	121
Bibliography	123

Illustrations Credits

Figure 2.1, Springer

Figure 2.2, Springer

Figure 2.3, Journal of Personality and Social Psychology

Figure 5.1, Éditions Denoël

Figure 5.2, Éditions Denoël

Figure 5.3, Éditions Du Dauphin

Figure 5.4, Éditions Du Dauphin

Figure 5.5, Aurora Press

Figure 5.6, Aurora Press

Figure 5.7, Éditions Denoël

Figure 5.8, Wiley

Figure 5.9, Urania Trust

Figure 5.10, The Journal of Social Psychology

Figure 5.11, The Journal of Social Psychology

Introduction

In the early 1990s, astrology seemed to me to be in a blind alley. I realize that at the time I was a little pessimistic about the future of this fascinating system of knowledge that had attracted my attention during my youth. If, on the one hand, I got highly satisfactory results, sometimes even surprising, on the other I felt a little frustrated. It lacked some consistency, more objective definitions, and more robust concepts. This of course did not include the low level of consensus among astrologers when interpreting an astrological chart. In some more recent sciences this problem also occurs, especially within the so-called human sciences. Unfortunately, in the case of astrology you don't see much willingness to question concepts, methods, and techniques. The validation of the knowledge also does not occupy a prominent position, and only recently, after more constant attacks by skeptics, has this become a worry for *a few* astrologers.

We will see in this book that, far from invalidating astrology, several studies made in the academic sphere draw our attention to the need for a deeper examination of the astrological phenomenon. Something as "exotic" as astrology causes almost hysterical reactions in the "harder" scientific environment. Usually any dialogue is discarded *a priori* because the mere interest in astrology is seen as absurd and ridiculous. In other cases, a willingness to evaluate it was simulated, but it soon became clear that it was just a badly disguised intention to prove "at any cost" that astrology is a superstition and must be eradicated. Nevertheless, there are studies in which the researcher sincerely tried to test astrological claims, apparently without prejudging them. However, we must recognize that even among those who systematically try to show that astrology is an illusion or a pseudoscience, as they like to call it, it is possible to draw valid and justifiable criticisms that, even though this was not the goal, fulfill the noble function of contributing to the improvement of astrological knowledge and also correcting its faults and inadequacies, which are not few.

Another problem often overlooked by researchers is the difference in language and concepts between psychology and astrology. When comparing the results of personality tests with interpretations of astrological charts, no effort is made to determine the appropriate connections, if any, between the astrological concepts and the concepts or constructs of the personality theory used. Psychologists and astrologers do not use the same language or, better still, they use entirely different paradigms and this must be taken into account. Not that the use of comparison is a waste of time, but if there was a previous attempt of interconceptual translation, we would probably not be facing what looks more like dialogue between Chinese and Yanomami.

Returning to my astrological road, there was a time when pessimism took hold of me. A flaw-riddled, apathetic, conservative, and nebulous astrology seemed to me to be unable to meet the challenges of the new century. It was during this critical phase that I met astrologer Carlos Fini. At the time I no longer read charts except at the insistence of acquaintances, friends, or relatives. Fini was then working with his partner, Yara Doarte, and both cultivated a healthy appreciation for both the scientific method and vision. This quality, more than desirable for an astrologer, was reflected in both the didactic activity carried out at the Hermes School and in the readings that they were providing for their clients. This contact was extremely important for the perspective that I would later adopt and that had for some time been germinating in my mind, and also for certain decisions I made concerning my involvement with astrology in this second phase. Fini and Doarte practiced an astrology that was serious, competent, lucid, and contemporaneous. Despite the name of the school, there was no place for wild esoteric thinking, or any thinking that mixed mysticism, astrology, and religion. Scientific knowledge and critical thinking were encouraged and the students learned an intelligent and objective kind of astrology.

Fini's ideas exerted a major influence on the work I have done for this book. They will always be mentioned here, when appropriate, as true arrows pointing out directions. His guidance was very important to the construction of a syntax that provides consistency and coherence to the astrological language. The free associations of more conventional readings, almost psychoanalytical, while highlighting the polysemy of astrological signs, end up multiplying their meanings to an almost infinite number. This makes the interpretation of a chart so subjective that its reproducibility becomes almost impossible. Therefore, the objectivity of astrology comes down to zero; in fact, there is no language, there is no way to establish a dialogue with contemporary science and therefore with the scientific culture of our time. Another important aspect of Fini's influence was the biological grounding of the astrological phenomenon. Understanding that there could be an interesting relationship between the triune brain theory of Paul MacLean and the astrological meanings of the planets, Fini shows us a very promising way to understand the physiological dimension that intermediates between planets and human personality.

The reader should already perceive that astrology is treated in a very unconventional way in this book. The focus of this book is not that of the fundamentalist skeptic or of the new age spiritualist. It's a risk taken on behalf of balance and fair measure; that is, I understand that both world views contain a specific bias that undermines an objective and dispassionate evaluation, as far as this is possible. Of both sides we observe a strong ideological commitment, full of emotion and fear that their beliefs and convictions shall crumble. At the same time, I do not believe in absolute objectivity or impartiality. I believe in the search for an ideal that, while unattainable, is desirable at all times. When I use the word "skeptic," it is better to say pseudo-skeptic, and the difference is clarified in this book. On the other hand, I am convinced that most people do not identify with either of these two extremes and therefore shall be open to the contents of this book.

It is very common for astrologers to seek in the distant past, in the mists of mythological thought, answers and explanations for the astrological phenomenon. The study of the origins of astrology, whether in civilizations that flourished in Mesopotamia, Hellenized Egypt, or even in Rome, is seen by many as key to understanding the mystery of the influence of the stars, or synchronicity between the macrocosm and microcosm. Some believe that there, in the past, they shall find the lost key that will finally answer all our questions. This search obviously refers to a belief in a revealed or intuitive knowledge that would be a privileged seizure of the truth. Of course after the truth comes decadence, confusion, and finally the "not-knowing," which is a characteristic of the present day, however much this may seem strange to more educated contemporary minds. At least this is what astrologers with esoteric motivation, mystical orientation, or something similar think.

Others, however, snub this occult discourse with no scientific or even rational basis. They prefer to cling to something more solid, more secure, which emanates from some authority of modern science. This authority exists, or rather existed, in Carl Gustav Jung, the first contemporary scientist to give some credence to astrology. For example, the Jungian concepts of *archetype* and *synchronicity* are widely used today by astrologers, as are the *psychological types*. But here also is projected the shadow of mysticism with which Jung felt quite comfortable. Traditionalist, reactionary, and romantic, the Swiss psychoanalyst always preferred the past to the present.

I do not follow either of these directions. The first, because it is a paradigm that has long been surpassed as a representation of the world, and the second, because of the inconsistency and fragility of its concepts, and of the vague discourse that barely disguises the author's ideology. Jung was very close to occult and esoteric thought, however eager to clinically validate ideas of a past that relentlessly haunted him. I do not believe the contemporary scientific spirit guided his steps. Rather, Jung hated the "modern" ideology of the academic world of his time. Therefore, I am committed to the scientific method, understanding that this is the best way to deal with natural, psychological, and social phenomena.

To establish the dialogue presented here, we need science and astrology to make use of a common method, or a language through which they can understand each other. If astrologers insist on disregarding the demands of a method that has been thoroughly tested over the centuries and that has brought many benefits for understanding the natural world and the human universe, it becomes impossible to make any kind of assessment. It is science that developed the appropriate tools for analysis and validation. I shall thus try to take the first steps to unravel the knots and bring these two perspectives together, thereby hoping that both parties will benefit.

The work presented here is limited to an approach to psychological astrology, and finding the link between psychology and astrology, or more precisely, between the trait theories and the astrological phenomenon. The main goal of this book is to build foundations for a more consistent reflection on the possibilities for validation of astrology. I think there are a lot of misconceptions about the nature of the astrological phenomenon. Discussions between skeptics and astrologers are not very enlightening and rarely do the two sides develop a constructive dialogue. Many of the claims of conventional or traditional astrology seem unreasonable, although its core, the correlation between celestial mechanics and something that could be considered as the structure of human personality or temperament, looms as a powerful indicator of this connection between human and celestial bodies. We must create conditions for the emergence of a new model, now an *astrological science*, whose concepts illuminate our understanding of the correlations that have been empirically observed throughout the centuries. It is also necessary to abandon many past beliefs in order to build a present that meets the demands of a secular society eager for projections in the future.

With new concepts that shall better describe the astrological phenomenon, defining them with clarity and precision and without the rancidity of magical thinking, mystical cloudiness, and hyperbolic esoteric fantasies, we can build a solid and reliable astrological foundation that will add relevant contributions to the understanding of new dimensions of life and their connections with nature.

ONE

Interpretation of the Birth Chart

The purpose of this chapter is not to teach the reader to interpret astrological charts, but to provide a brief introduction to the mainstream of astrology. There are of course other lines of thought in present day astrology, more traditional orientations and methods that follow different paths. I believe, however, that an astrology that often draws on Jungian theory, at least in some of its assumptions, is today the most widely accepted and used in the West. I will spare the reader the psychoanalytic complexities because these theories are not always clarified in astrological analysis. In addition, a brief reading of a chart such as the one at the end of this chapter does not require it. My intention is only to show how the astrologer works with the main variables in order to create a psychological profile.

What is an Astrological Chart?

The natal chart, also called the birth chart, radical chart, or horoscope, is a graphical representation of the sky at the time and place of an individual's birth. Astrology does not only analyze charts of people; it also deals with charts of nations, cities, companies, enterprises, and any event whose beginning can be determined in time and space. This book only discusses individuals and their psychological profiles.

In order to calculate a natal chart you must know where the person was born, the location and longitude and latitude of the place of birth, and the date and time of birth (preferably from a birth certificate or record, not the mother's memory). Inaccuracies of up to four or five minutes, or even ten, *usually* do not invalidate the work of the astrologer. In some forecasting techniques, an error of

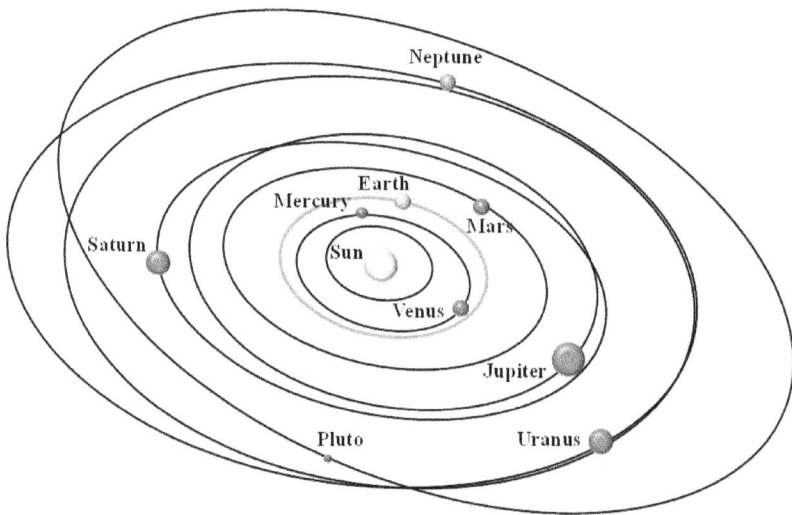

Figure 1.1 The Solar System

four minutes or more makes a difference, although it is possible to rectify a birth time using astrological techniques. Corrections for errors that are more than ten or twelve minutes are not reliable, and anything more than that might be impossible to rectify.

Every conventional chart shows the positions in the zodiacal circle of the planets of the solar system (see Figure 1.1)–Mercury, Venus, Mars, Jupiter, Saturn, Uranus, Neptune, and Pluto (downgraded by astronomers to dwarf-planet status), as well as the Sun and Moon, which in astrology are called planets. In their orbits, these celestial bodies are distributed in the twelve signs of the zodiac. Superimposed on the sign division there is another division: the astrological houses, which are also twelve in number. The first house begins with the Ascendant. The zodiac is a band of 16 degrees of arc in the sky, where an observer on Earth can see the orbit of the astrological planets. The zodiac circle has its center in the ecliptic, which is the plane of the Sun's apparent orbit around the Earth. We know, of course, that it is actually the Earth that revolves around the Sun and therefore the ecliptic is the plane of Earth's orbit. But in both astrology and astronomy, Earth is the reference point. The positions of the planets in the zodiac are thus a projection of their orbits in this imaginary circle, as seen from Earth.

Along the ecliptic we find the twelve zodiacal constellations that gave their names to the signs of the zodiac, plus the constellation Ophiuchus, which is also cut by the ecliptic. Because of this some people say that there should be thirteen signs rather than twelve. This comes from a misunderstanding of the difference between a zodiac sign and a constellation. They are different things and bear no relationship to each other, except for their names.

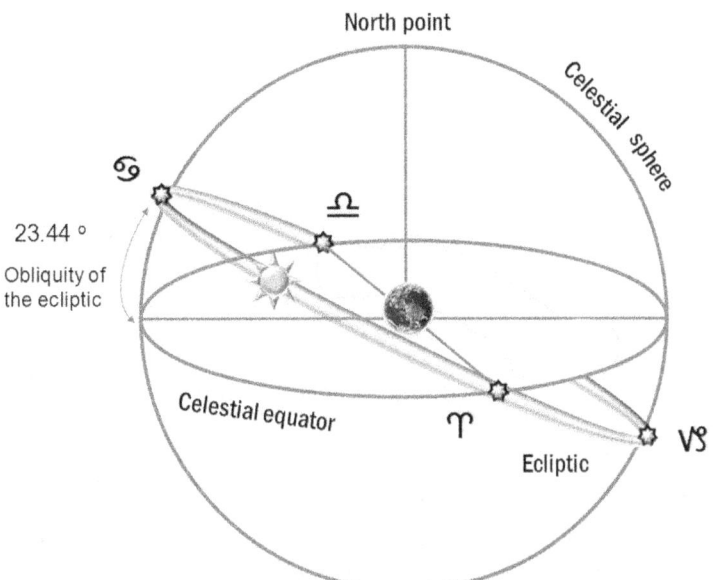

Figure1.2 Celestial Sphere with the Eclipitic and Celestial Equator

If we imagine, from our terrestrial point of view, that we occupy the center of a giant celestial sphere (Figure 1.2), and from any point on our planet we can see the top half of that sphere and the celestial equator, a projection of the Earth's equator onto the celestial sphere. The ecliptic and the celestial equator intersect at two points: the vernal equinoctial point, which is 0 Aries, and the autumn equinox, or 0 Libra. The first marks the passage of the Sun from the celestial southern hemisphere to the northern hemisphere, and the second from north to south, in the apparent movement of this star in the sky.

The Ascendant, a virtual point in space that marks the intersection of the horizon of the birth place and the ecliptic, is the same in every house system. In most house systems this point marks the beginning of the first house. The Descendant is the point opposite the Ascendant, or the beginning of the seventh house. In the house system most commonly used in Western astrology, the Placidus system, the intersection between the local meridian (an imaginary circle perpendicular to the local horizon that passes through the north and south points) and the ecliptic marks the Midheaven, usually the beginning of the tenth house, or the degree of culmination, the point at which the Sun crosses the meridian at noon; on the opposite side, below the horizon, is the Bottom of the Sky, or IC, the point that usually marks the beginning of the fourth house. The cusps (beginning) of the intermediate houses vary according to the house system used.

The positions of the planets in the zodiac signs are listed in an ephemeris designed for astrological work. Astrological software is most often used to calculate the chart. Then the chart can be interpreted.

Planets

Each planet has a distinct meaning, expressing a series of correlations with specific human qualities and with certain categories of objects and activities. A planet rules one or two signs and in these signs its potential can manifest or develop more fully. When a planet occupies one of these signs, it is in its domicile; that is, it is at home, a place where it has more strength. Each planet also occupies one of the twelve houses. The main psychological meanings of the planets are as follows:

Sun, rules Leo: power, authority, leadership, accomplishment, success, progress, vitality, generosity, creativity, pride.

Moon, rules Cancer: instincts and emotions, the mother, maternity, receptivity, imagination, fluctuations, uncertainties.

Mercury, rules Gemini and Virgo: intellect, thought, perception, communication, information, learning.

Venus, rules Taurus and Libra: love, affection, relationships, pleasure, sociability, esthetic sense.

Mars, rules Aries and Scorpio: action, strength, impulse, competition, desire, sexual energy.

Jupiter, rules Sagittarius and Pisces: optimism, outgoing nature, cheerfulness, extraversion, enthusiasm, philosophical tendencies.

Saturn, rules Capricorn and Aquarius: discipline, responsibility, organization, consolidation, construction, caution, patience, introversion, fear.

Uranus, rules Aquarius: freedom, independence, originality, eccentricity, individualism, rebellion.

Neptune, rules Pisces: inspiration, spirituality, enchantment, illusions, ideals, artistic tendencies.

Pluto, rules Scorpio: the unconscious, profound transformations, obsessions, destructive tendencies, losses, abandonment, control, domination, manipulation.

Aspects

Some angular distances (the aspects) between the planets are significant; they show the quality of the astrological relationship between them. The major aspects are:

Conjunction: 0 degrees

Sextile: 60 degrees

Square: 90 degrees

Trine: 120 degrees

Opposition: 180 degrees

The square and opposition are tense and/or negative aspects; the sextile and trine are facilitators and/or positive. A conjunction is neutral.

Signs

The twelve signs of the zodiac are divided into four categories: fire, earth, air, and water. These are called the four elements or triplicities. Fire is intuitive/enthusiastic, earth is pragmatic, air is intellectual/communicative, and water is emotional. The signs are also divided according to quality or modality: cardinal signs (Aries, Cancer, Libra, and Capricorn) are sociable and take initiative; fixed signs (Taurus, Leo, Scorpio, and Aquarius) are rigid, and mutable signs (Gemini, Virgo, Sagittarius and Pisces) are flexible. The earth and water signs are classified as feminine or negative, and the air and fire signs as masculine or positive. This is a polarity relationship.

Below is a brief description of each of the signs in terms of personality traits.

Aries: dynamic, courageous, imprudent, impulsive, aggressive, impatient, rash, selfish.

Taurus: patient, persistent, determined, stable, inflexible, obstinate, possessive, sensual, slow.

Gemini: versatile, adaptable, communicative, witty, eloquent, inconsistent, shrewd, inquiring.

Cancer: emotional, affectionate, imaginative, protective, attached to the family, inconstant, susceptible, sensitive.

Leo: authoritarian, domineering, proud, vain, dramatic, generous, creative, loyal.

Virgo: modest, meticulous, methodic, perfectionist, skeptical, analytical, critical, diligent, demanding.

Libra: cooperative, diplomatic, friendly, impartial, balanced, persuasive, hesitant, refined.

Scorpio: determined, obsessive, tough, self-controlled, intuitive, passionate, suspicious, reserved.

Sagittarius: optimistic, enthusiastic, jovial, tolerant, philosophical, hedonistic, prone to exaggerate.

Capricorn: cautious, disciplined, responsible, pessimistic, conventional, discreet, inhibited.

Aquarius: original, inventive, independent, individualistic, rebel, progressive, unpredictable, eccentric.

Pisces: receptive, supportive, empathetic, compassionate, impressionable, introspective, melancholy, confused.

It is common to find overlapping of meanings in the signs. Certain traits, qualities, or characteristics can be true to two or more signs, a fact that is clarified in the next chapter.

Houses

Each of the houses represents a sphere of human life or field of experience with its various relevant activities. These are conceptual spaces that manifest the meanings of the astrological chart. There is an analogy between the meanings of the first sign (Aries) and the first house, the second sign (Taurus) and the second house, the third sign (Gemini) and the third house, and so on.

First House (Ascendant): personality, temperament, individuality, way of expression, attitude, the body, physical appearance, health.

Second House: resources and material goods, possessions, money, gains and losses, sense of security and values.

Third House: communication, exchange of information, learning, short journeys, means of transport, the neighborhood, brothers and sisters.

Fourth House: the home, house, family, parents, home country, property, the last years of life.

Fifth House: sons and daughters, children, entertainment, games, pleasures, dating, creativity, artistic performance.

Sixth House: work relationships, job, subordinates, pets, routines, health.

Seventh House: societies, partnerships, negotiations, contracts, commitments, marriage, interpersonal relationships in general.

Eighth House: death, surgeries, physical harm, inheritance, investment, regeneration, sex, research and investigations, secrets.

Ninth House: higher education, long journeys, foreign countries, ideals, laws, ethical questions, religion, public opinion.

Tenth House (Midheaven): profession, social status, aspirations, ambitions, reputation, authorities.

Eleventh House: social life, social conscience, friends, objectives, hopes.

Twefth House: the unconscious, reclusion, isolation, limitations, frustrations, weaknesses, chronic illnesses, social institutions.

Interpretation

There are many methods and styles of interpretation in contemporary astrology. Contrary to what skeptics think, this does not work against the objectivity of astrologers, nor turn astrology into chaos. The diversity of approaches is always enriching and welcome. The problem is not there but in the ineffectiveness of some methods and concepts that are often vague and inconsistent. The best interpretations can establish a psychological profile with reasonable success even though they are left wanting when faced by the demands of objective psychology as a science. I believe that by resolving some mistakes and using operational concepts, which entail a greater methodological rigor, it is possible to develop high standards of analysis.

To get a rough idea of how a competent Western astrologer would interpret a client's natal chart, below is list of variables that are usually included. This list is a guideline, not something that covers all the aspects of the subject.

General configurations are:

- 1. The number of planets above and below the horizon, and to the east and west of the meridian.
- 2. Chart pattern (according to the distribution of planets in the zodiac).
- 3. The dominant triplicity. Does an element predominate?
- 4. The dominant quality. Does a quality predominate?
- 5. Polarity.

Specific configurations are:

- 6. Sun: sign, house and aspects
- 7. Moon: sign, house and aspects
- 8. Ascendant: sign, planets in conjunction (or other aspect), planets in the house
- 9. Planet that rules the Ascendant (ruler of the chart): sign, house, aspects
- 10. Midheaven: sign, planets in conjunction, planets in the house
- 11. The remaining planets: sign, house, and aspects

Interperetation, called synthesis, sounds complicated and indeed it can be. There are so many variables that the astrologer needs to be organized in order to develop an interpretation that is consistent and of course that accurately describes the personality of the client. The steps listed above are a simplification of the work to be done. To understand how the astrologer works, there is nothing better than an example.

Guimarães Rosa (Fig. 3.1) was an extraordinarily creative writer, multi-linguist, physician, and diplomat who had diverse interests throughout his life. A polyvalent man, Rosa worked with language in a daring and highly original way. His complete works are a plunge to the depths of the human soul. But it's not just any plunge; it is one that brings enchantment, vertigo, amazement, and pleasure. Reading the work of Guimarães Rosa is an unforgettable aesthetic experience.

According to the criteria above, the following is a list of the factors used in reading Rosa's chart:

1. There are six planets below the horizon, four above, indicating that he is a little more introverted, just slightly turned inward. Nine planets in the east side of the chart means he is not easily influenced and that he has well defined opinions.

2. The chart is a Bucket shape, with nine planets occupying half of the map, and the remaining planet in the other half. The singleton planet is the handle of the bucket, the channel of expression of the energy accumulated on the other side. This planet, Uranus in the seventh house, indicates creativity, originality, and socially projected eccentricity. He wants to make his mark with singularity.

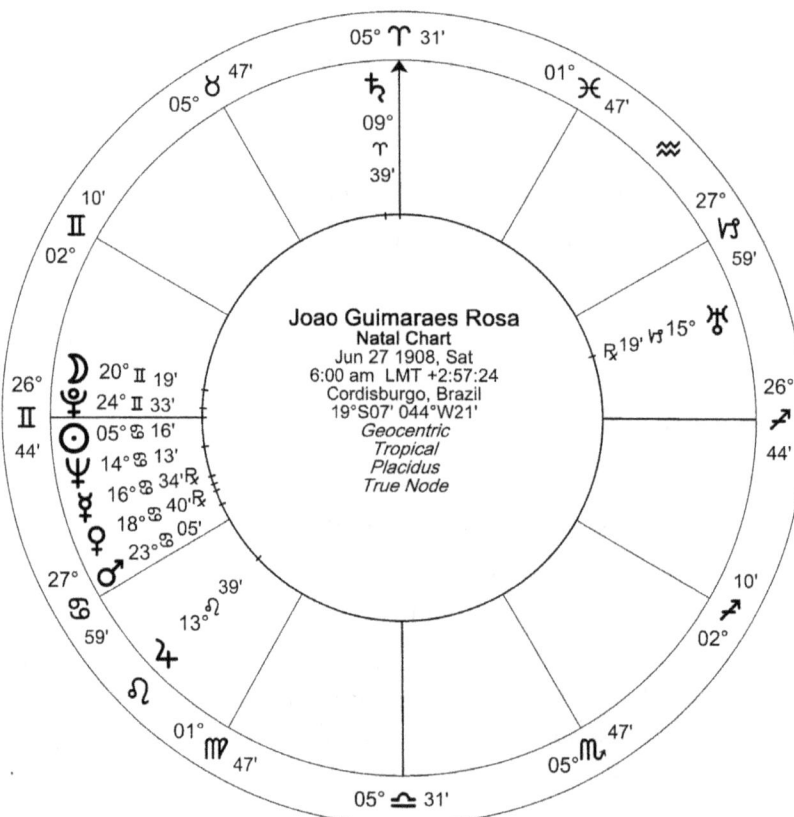

Figure 1.3 João Guimarães Rosa's Natal Chart.

3. The water element predominates. He is quite emotional. With a deficit in the earth element, he lacks practicality and has difficulty in coping with day-to-day reality.

4. Cardinal signs predominate, so he is a sociable man with a lot of initiative. A deficit in fixed signs indicates dispersion and a lack of focus and objectivity.

5. The polarity is balanced.

6. Regarding the Sun, he is highly emotional and nostalgic, attached to family, the past, traditions, and birthplace. He is proud and authoritarian with a sharp sensitivity, vivid imagination, artistic and/or mystical inclinations, creative, original, unconventional, and maybe a little eccentric. At the same time, in many ways he is conservative and worries what people think about him, alternating between boldness and caution. Old things probably fascinate him.

7. Regarding the Moon, his feelings and emotions fluctuate. He is attracted by a wide range of stimuli and is unstable and ambivalent, witty and playful. He has strong passions, is possessive, and frequently needs to be alone.

8. Regarding the Ascendant, he is talkative, versatile, curious, and eager for knowledge and information. He is articulate, restless, and likes to discuss things and do several things at once. He has a quick wit and is shrewd and perceptive, but finds it difficult make decisions. He lives at a fast pace, and sometimes he is authoritarian and controlling.

9. Regarding the chart ruler, Mercury, his focus is on his own emotions, on the intimacy of his own feelings. Relationship with family is fundamental, and he appreciates the poetic and/or mystical dimension of life. A probable searcher for the unusual and the unconventional, he is creative and original.

10. Regarding the Midheaven, he is a person of great initiative in the professional sphere, and has difficulty accepting subordinate positions. He is determined and courageous in making decisions in the professional environment, and seeks to impose his will, but without excess. There could be major conflicts between his personality and his profession, between the social image he wants to project and the work he performs.

11. Regarding the remaining planets, the three personal planets (Mercury, Venus, and Mars) are in Cancer and the first house. He has a keen imagination, holds on to the past and traditions, and often relies more on intuition than analysis. Even so, critical thinking tends to be well developed. He is highly creative and might be unconventional in some of his ideas. He is affectionate, romantic, sentimental, and zealous in love relationships. At the same time, he is mindful to safeguard his freedom and independence. He can understand the feminine soul. In his perception, sexuality and love easily merge.

Report

If João Guimarães Rosa were to consult an astrologer, he would receive a psychological profile analysis similar to the following:

> João Guimarães Rosa has his own ideas and opinions and is not easily influenced by others. His tends to be unconventional. More than that, he seems to want to show his originality and creativity to others. So he is probably seen as an odd or strange person, as well as independent and rebellious. He is preoccupied, with an intense focus on himself that can be an inward search or an acute narcissism.
>
> Extremely sensitive, emotional, and imaginative, he is strongly attached to family and the comfort of his home. He is also attached to things of the past, the place where he was born, his origins. There is a clear internal conflict between the creative and original and a strictly conservative bias of his personality. This makes him alternate between courage and boldness, and caution and prudence.
>
> Dealing with day-to-day practical matters is not always easy for him, and he often lacks objectivity in dealing with the pragmatic dimension of life. He feels more comfortable with the abstract world of ideas and arguments, but socially he is

witty, good-humored, playful, and communicative. Articulate and with a great need to share his thoughts with others, he has the ability to discuss the most diverse subjects, even when he is unfamiliar with the topic of conversation.

The breadth of his interests is therefore quite extensive. He always tries to be well informed and probably likes to read or at least watch the news of the day. He is inconstant and perhaps ambiguous in his attitudes and positions in life. Anyway, his flexibility and versatility imply wit and cunning. But he finds it difficult to make up his mind and make decisions.

Affectionate and friendly, loving and sentimental, nostalgic and insecure, he is also a proud and relatively authoritarian man, controlling and domineering, with a tendency to covet and seek positions of power and prestige in society. We can highlight, moreover, his need to protect and engage people in a strong affective network, which also serves to give him more security.

In terms of affection, one can say that he is romantic and easily falls in love, but also cherishes his independence, which can make him quite fickle. Either way, his intention, his disposition, is to form bonds and not just live adventures.

Because there is not really a biography of Guimarães Rosa, just some information scattered here and there, we lack any comparison. The goal here, however, is not to confirm the accuracy of the analysis, but to in a few words describe how an interpretation is constructed from the elements or variables in the chart. As already stated, this is a simplification, and many details were omitted. However, I believe that this overview of an astrological interpretation is enough to get an idea of what an astrologer does when interpreting the astrological chart of a client.

In the following chapters I will try to justify a different course for astrology, which is not exactly the negation of what we have just seen, but a re-conceptualization and overcoming of various problems that hinder the development of astrological knowledge. This will mean moving in the direction of the scientific method, aiming at an open and frank dialogue with contemporary science.

Two

Trait Theories: Rescuing a Tradition

One of the ideas I advocate in this book is the purely subjective nature of the astrological chart. This ancient representation of the sky at birth allows us to read not much more than the dynamics of personality traits. Or, better yet, it gives us access to the structure of the human temperament, which can be understood as the psychobiological core from and around which the personality develops. Thus the influences of the social environment do not act on a totally malleable *tabula rasa*, as the behaviorists believed. There are innate predispositions that typically respond to external stimuli. The temperament is part of these predispositions and the personality is the result, relatively stable, of the interaction nature-environment. It's most likely that astrology reveals the content of the temperament but does not include the total personality, which is larger and more comprehensive. This means rejecting the psychoanalytic interpretations of astrology, especially Jungian, which virtually see a reflection of the personality in the astrological chart, and necessarily, of experiences that will be lived through.

Now that we have defined the focus of an astrological analysis of a psychological profile, we must deal with the concept of personality trait. What a trait is, how it emerges in the dynamics of a natal chart and how to test the astrological hypothesis relative to the trait are questions I attempt to answer in this chapter. After all, the goal is to know what the chart depicts and how it depicts. What is a trait and what are its astrological implications? This is the first question to be answered.

In this chapter I present the main trait theories, whose historical roots date from the distant doctrine of Galen's four temperaments, the common source of all of the typological theories that later emerged in the West. Committed to the old metaphysical concepts and often ignoring the systematic observation of the scientific method, psychological astrology took another direction, got lost on the way and became tangled in speculative deductions and mystical and esoteric ingredients. The questions are: How do we recover this trajectory and propose possible corrections, orienting ourselves with the methods used in today's various trait theories? Ultimately, how do we lay the groundwork for a dialogue between two knowledge systems that are so different? These are questions I will attempt to answer after demonstrating the common historical origin of psychological astrology and trait theories.

From the Four Elements to the Four Temperaments

The Greek philosophical tradition cites Empedocles of Agrigentum as the creator of the doctrine of the four elements, and it was mainly due to this idea that he became known as a pre-Socratic thinker, physician, and politician. A most eccentric figure, Empedocles lived between 490 and 435 BC. He had a most inflated self-concept, considered himself a god and a prophet, and thus attracted followers wherever he went. He was the author of two poems, *On the Nature* and *Purifications*. For him, fire, earth, air and water were the four roots, or *rhizomata*, that all matter was composed of. These roots were indestructible, immutable, and eternal. The term elements only began to be used later by other philosophers. According to Empedocles, the aggregation of fire, earth, air and water occurs thanks to a principle he called Love (Philotis). The segregation is through the work of another principle, Strife or Hatred (Neikos). Therefore, Love and Strife are the two antagonistic principles which, acting upon the four elements, generate movement and change, enabling combinations responsible for shaping the world as we know it.

By the way, roots was a term used by Pythagoras, in whom Empedocles probably was inspired to formulate his ideas. Followers of Pythagoras believed in the divine character of numbers as the very expression of universal order, that numerical ratios are the essence of everything in the world, and that matter was an expression of the number four. Such belief takes us back to the four roots of Empedocles as the basis of the material world. In fact, this philosopher believed that the quality of the matter depended on the proportion of root elements that constitute it. They were four in number, and the difference between a tree trunk, a flower petal, a rock, and the wing of a bat depended on the quantity of each of the four elements that is necessary to constitute these various natural objects. It's all a matter of specific combinations, a quality emerging as an expression of quantity.

A contemporary of Empedocles, the philosopher and physician Alcmaeon of Croton (c. 510-440 BC) presented some ideas that would be critical to the future doctrine of the four elements and other quaternary theories such as the four humors and the four temperaments. For him, all disease arose from a condition of imbalance between opposing qualities, such as hot and cold, dry and wet, sweet and bitter, or qualities considered "forces" that make up the body mass. The equalization or balance between these pairs of opposites promotes health, while the imbalance, or monarchy, as he called it, causes disease. For some authors, Alcmaeon had also been influenced by the Pythagoreans, or even by Pythagoras himself, who arrived in Croton around 530 BC. For others, he was not exactly a Pythagorean, but his ideas at some point converged with those of Pythagoras and his followers. In the fragments concerning Alcmaeon's ideas, we can identify the influence of the early Ionian philosophers, notably those regarding the idea of the balance of opposites, formulated by Anaximander.

These ideas were incorporated into ancient Greek medicine, which then began to move away from magical practices as the Greeks started a search for rational answers to questions about the nature of things. And these answers should now be found in nature. This is what, for example, the philosophers of the Ionian school of thought did, starting a philosophical study that was not focused on the gods or mythology but on the physical essence of all that exists. This rationalism had also been embraced by the Hippocrateans, who dismissed mystical and religious explanations for disease and illness and rejected the use of magic to cure illness. Treatment and causality belong to the realm of rationality.

The reference to the Hippocrateans concerns a broad medical tradition that includes the various authors of the *Corpus Hippocraticum*, among them the most important of all, Hippocrates of Kos. There are about sixty medical treaties that were written in Ionic dialect at the end of the fifth century and early fourth century BC. It is a heterogeneous corpus, often presenting opposing ideas, but one that consolidates a naturalistic view of organic processes. In Hippocratic medicine, the relationship of humans with the environment–the position of the stars, the seasons, climate, geographical location, and wind–is of extreme importance. In *On the Nature of Man*, a Hippocratic text that Aristotle attributed to Polybius, Hippocrates' son-in-law, the theory of the four humors is introduced, which is of particular interest for the purposes of this chapter. According to the author, nature expresses a quaternary rhythm that generates four qualities, four elements, four cardinal points, four ages in the life of a human being, and four humors in the body: blood, phlegm, yellow bile, and black bile. It is worth saying that before Hippocrates, ancient Greek medicine was already based on humor diagnosis and even the *Corpus Hippocraticum* gives us more than one theory of humors.

In the humoural theory that appears in *On the Nature of Man*, the four humours presented the following correspondences (see Table 2.1): Blood is linked to the air element, whose qualities are warm and moist, and prevails in spring and during childhood. Yellow bile represents the fire element, with warm and dry qualities that predominate in summer and during youth. Black bile is associated with the earth element; its qualities are cold and dry and prevail in autumn and adulthood. Phlegm reflects the water element with the qualities of cold and moist, which prevail in winter and in old age. This was the basis of Galen's first draft centuries later of what would later be the theory of the four temperaments: sanguine, choleric, melancholic and phlegmatic.

For the Hippocrateans, disease was the result of an imbalance in the ratio of these humours in the body. Curing the disease was thus restoring the balance disturbed by humoural imbalance, whose causes were natural: the "air" of the place, the change of the seasons, or the person's own excesses. Now what really mattered was to observe the patient and his/her behavior, which was not relevant when accepting supernatural causes that were unattainable for mere mortals. This paradigm shift

Table 2.1 The Four Elements and Their Correspondences				
Element	*Qualities*	*Humour*	*Season*	*Age*
Air	Warm, moist	Blood	Spring	Childhood
Fire	Warm, dry	Yellow bile	Summer	Youth
Earth	Cold, dry	Black bile	Autumn	Adulthood
Water	Cold, moist	Phlegm	Winter	Old age

occurred in the context of a wave of rationality that swept the Greek world and laid the foundations of Western thought and science. The historical moment in which this new perspective appears is the classical period of Athenian democracy (or just before), the so-called era of Pericles, and other such figures as Sophocles, Euripides, Democritus, Socrates, Thucydides, Phidias and other Greek intellectuals. Both Alcmaeon and the Hippocratic doctors were influenced by early pre-Socratic philosophers and the great innovation that they brought with them: the search for natural causes for equally natural phenomena. The gods and their whims leave the stage, at least as an explanation for what naturally happens in the world. Observing things, the philosopher tries to learn the order and the cause and effect underlying mere sensory perception.

It is important to note that philosophical thought and empirical and rational medicine emerged at about the same historical moment as the emerging *polis* and, later, democracy in Greece. This new political ideology that developed in Greek society allowed and promoted discussion, debate, and dissemination of ideas. Any citizen (women, slaves, and foreigners were excluded) could express an opinion on matters of public interest. The thinking that predominated was that of the person who best knew how to convince his peers with logical and rational argument. The people no longer had the absolute authority of the king or a warrior aristocracy hanging over them but that which was written in laws made by citizens themselves and known by all. These were the necessary social conditions for the free development and circulation of ideas, the culture in which doctrines and theories competed in an attempt to explain the world without the imposition of mythical thought and without the tyrannical omnipresence of the gods, who were not totally discarded but relegated to a background role. The *physis*, nature, is self-regulating, and it is there that the ordering principles and origin of all things, including living beings, must be sought. Also emphasized were the pioneering thoughts of the early Ionian philosophers, like Thales, Anaximander and Anaximenes.

The activities of anthropomorphic gods were replaced by natural principles that were, themselves, divine. The whole of nature became divine, something the Hippocratic doctors recognized in their treaties. As they advocated natural causes for disease, they made all nature sacred. It was not, however, a materialistic thought but a vision of order and regularity perceived in the world of senses and to which was attributed a divine character. This was quite different from the injunctions of anthropomorphic gods who, on a whim, interfered in the world, whether by causing disease or disasters such as earthquakes or floods.

We have seen that the Pythagorean concepts of quaternity and harmony, the isonomy and the qualities of Alcmaeon, and the doctrine of the four elements of Empedocles all helped to build the theory of four humours that appears in the Hippocratic treatise *On the Nature of Man*, and that formed the basis for the later emergence of the four temperaments theory. But none of this would be possible without the paradigm revolution introduced by early pre-Socratic Ionian School and the political innovation engendered in Greece with the emergence of the *polis* and democracy, socio-political conditions that were extremely important for the development of free thought. Without the chains of a forceful and dogmatic priestly caste, the rationality that was emerging in the Ionian and in the Pythagorean and other pre-Socratic philosophical speculations enabled the development of natural medicine and later of a proto-psychology with a physiological basis–the theory of the four temperaments–that was initiated by Galen and later developed by other authors.

In the *Corpus Hippocraticum* we can see an attempt to relate physical characteristics and behavior, which then would become the science of physiognomy. Mental illness also received naturalistic explanations, such as the so-called "sacred disease," epilepsy, at the time attributed to the act of a god who wanted to punish the individual. But for the Hippocratic authors it was just an illness like any other, whose cause was in the brain. Gradually, adjectives like "blood," "bilious," and "phlegmatic" began to be used to describe behavior and psychological characteristics.

The Hippocrateans said nothing about astrology. They just made allusions to the need for physicians to learn astronomy in order to define the rising and setting of the stars and asterisms. Sirius, Arcturus, and the Pleiades are mentioned, but this type of observation is an ancient one in Greece and can be attested to in Hesiod and Homer. It does not involve astrology. The earliest references on Greek authors who had knowledge of Babylonian astrology, such as Eudoxus of Cnidus and Theophrastus, are from the fourth century BC, the same time frame of the books of Hippocratic medicine, which reflect a consolidated and established tradition. The first record of the theory of the four elements in astrology appears in Book IV of the *Anthology* of Vettius Valens in the second century AD. Ptolemy, his contemporary and author of *Tetrabiblos*, despite mentioning the four triplicities arranged in the form of four triangles, makes no mention of the elements; he mentions only the qualities: hot, cold, wet, and dry. Manilius, a little more than a century earlier, around 10 AD, referred to the trigonal division of signs, distributing them in four categories of three signs each. The four elements, however, fail to be associated with this division, although in Book I of *Astronomica* they appear as the elements that form the universe. In these three authors we therefore find the same divisions of triplicities:

- Fire: Aries, Leo and Sagittarius
- Earth: Taurus, Virgo and Capricorn
- Air: Gemini, Libra and Aquarius
- Water: Cancer, Scorpio and Pisces

According to Rochberg-Halton, the trigonal division of the signs of the zodiac was known to the

Babylonians even though it had not been associated with the idea of different qualities or four elements, which was a Greek invention. The signs of the zodiac were grouped in the same way as they later appear in Hellenistic astrology, whose distribution corresponds to the four primary elements that form the world: fire, earth, air and water. Moreover, since the seventh century BC there was a similar grouping involving the twelve months of the solar year, and in the late astrological text *TCL 6 13*, what you see is a circle with four triangles. Therefore, resulting from the original idea that divides the zodiac into four groups of three signs, the Greeks simply attributed to these ternaries the elements of Empedocles, which were already part of a cosmological theory that had been well developed by Aristotle and widely accepted among the scholars of the time.

In *Of the Natural Faculties*, Galen (129-200 AD), a physician born in Pergamum who later moved to Rome, following the Hippocratic tradition, combined the four qualities (hot and cold, wet and dry) to compose the four humours, but without directly using the concept of four elements. In the treatise *On the Temperaments*, he shows how the excess of one of the qualities, which produces humoral imbalance, brings out the four temperaments: sanguine, phlegmatic, choleric, and melancholic. The ideal temperament would be one in which the four qualities were in perfect balance or *eucrasia*, without any excesses, thereby positioning the individual at the midpoint between ". . . boldness and timidity, negligence and impertinence, compassion and envy . . ." (Stalikas and Stelmack, 1991). The qualities varied along the main cold-wet and hot-dry axis, also indicating the emphasized element. If there were, for example, an imbalance favoring qualities like cold and dry, pointing to the earth element, the result would be an excess of black bile and melancholy temperament. If, on the other hand, the qualities of hot and dry predominated, associated with the fire element, the excess yellow bile induced a choleric temperament. It is interesting to see, however, that according to Galen, phlegm, contrary to blood, yellow bile, and black bile, was not responsible for a specific character, and so for him there was no phlegmatic temperament, which only later was included in the system. The so-called doctrine or theory of the four temperaments was not totally developed in Galen, and only later would take the form we know today. It's at the end of the ancient world and throughout the Middle Ages that a more consistent and comprehensive description of the four temperaments was created and included and consolidated in the astrological system.

In *Prognostication of Disease by Astrology* and *The Critical Days*, Galen points out the influence of the Moon in the astrological signs of the zodiac and its aspects to other planets, besides the prediction of disease that affects the individual, the treatment to be used and also whether the patient will die. This knowledge he attributed to "Egyptian astronomers." Nevertheless, Galen condemned horoscopes, i.e., genethliac astrology, although he accepted the influence of planets and stars on the human body.

Traits and Types

Still in the eighteenth century, the theory of the four temperaments enjoyed great prestige among doctors and philosophers, which is why it was taught in universities. The physiological determination of character was widely accepted and it seemed a quite natural and sensible explanation.

In 1798, philosopher Immanuel Kant published *Anthropology from a Pragmatic Point of View*, a book based on notes from his annual lectures on anthropology given between 1776 and 1792. In the section that deals with the character of the person, Kant, from a more descriptive than causal perspective, presents the characteristics of each of the temperaments, first dividing them in two classes, feeling and activity, and then in strong or weak. Sanguine and melancholic are feeling temperaments, the first strong (and short) and the second weak (and lasting). Choleric and phlegmatic temperaments are both activity temperaments, the first intense, but not persistent, and the second not very active, but durable. As a result there are four independent temperaments without any combination that would generate intermediate states.

It can be said that the sanguine type is the astrological equivalent of a predominance of air in the chart, and described by Kant as one who has many friends and is carefree, hopeful, impatient, helpful, not very firm, sociable, playful, and capricious, and does not take things too seriously or make much effort. The melancholic type, equivalent to an emphasis on the earth element, is anxious, pessimistic, responsible, concerned, suspicious, and brooding, with a tendency for sadness. The choleric type, which predominates in the fire element, is irritable, active, proud, avaricious, refined, and easily excitable, does not bear a grudge, lacks persistence, and likes to give orders and attract attention. Kant says the fire type is the least happy because these people attract many enemies. The phlegmatic, whose emphasis is on the water element, is cold, inclines toward inactivity and indolence, takes time to get excited but remains excited for a longer period, and is not easily provoked.

In the late nineteenth century, the experimentalist Wilhelm Wundt, one of the fathers of modern psychology, focused on the traditional model of the four temperaments, adjusting them to two varying principles of reactivity: the strength of feelings or emotions and the speed with which they vary or change. Choleric and melancholic people tend to experience strong emotions; phlegmatic and sanguine types are prone to weak emotions. In terms of changeability, sanguine and choleric types change rapidly, and phlegmatic and melancholic types are slow to change. Wundt believed that this ancient four-fold division was the result of keen observations between people; hence its empirical validity. Wundt's scheme, according to Eysenck, brings innovation, which is a quantitative variation along two dimensions (strength and changeability of emotions) and the possibility of combinations, forming a normal distribution. This is in contrast to the temperaments, which are compartmentalized categories in which the individual is labeled as a phlegmatic, melancholic, choleric, or sanguine type. Wundt, unlike Kant, does not postulate the existence of four distinct types. Along the two principles or dimensions, one can occupy any position. Bringing together these two authors, Eysenck and Eysenck (1985) present the scheme shown in Figure 2.1.

Continuing the idea of temperament, Swiss psychiatrist Carl Gustav Jung, in *Psychological Types*, constructs a speculative typological psychology from the concepts of attitude and psychological function. For him, extraversion and introversion are the two attitudes or dispositions of the personality that orient the individual, respectively, to the outside (to the object) or to the inner or subjective sphere. The extravert is led by objective conditions and circumstances that become de-

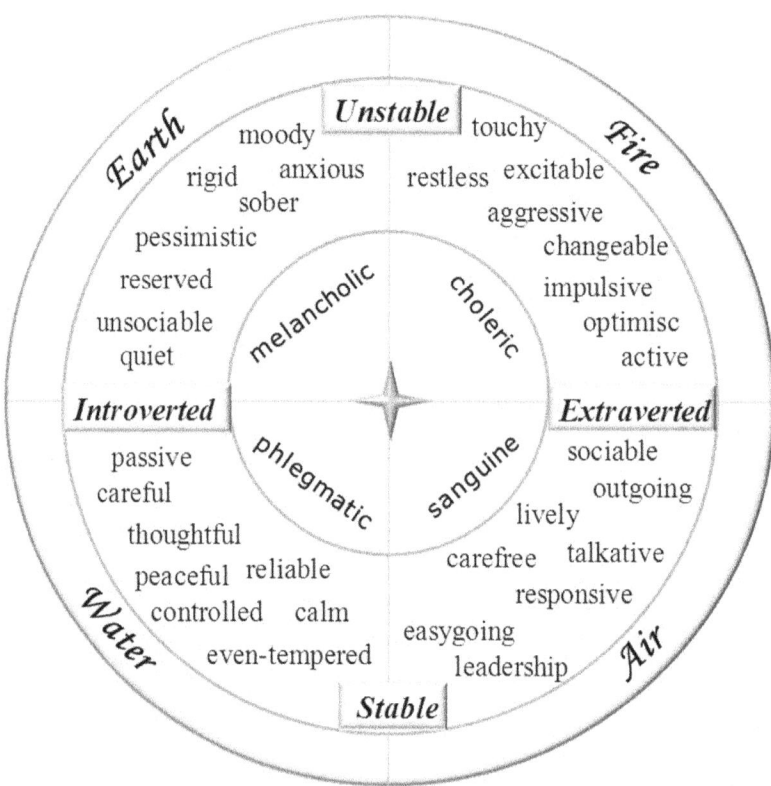

Figure 2.1 The Four Temperaments and the Four Elements (modified from Eysenck and Eysenck, 1985).

terminants of behavior. He or she is highly influenced by the external world, easily yielding to the demands of the environment. The orientation toward the object is, therefore, the extraverted person's hallmark.

The opposite is true with the introvert. His or her orientation is toward the self and this sets a priority on the subjective relationship to the world and his or her world view. This is what we call external locus of control and internal locus of control, respectively.

According to Jung, there are four psychological functions: thinking, feeling, sensation, and intuition. Having said that he had come to these functions "on a purely empirical bases," Jung combined these functions and attitudes of extraversion and introversion, generating eight basic personality types: extraverted thinking, extraverted feeling, extraverted sensing, extraverted intuitive, introverted thinking, introverted feeling, introverted sensing and introverted intuitive. These types are habitual dispositions, i.e., individual characteristics that appear with regularity. In each type attitudes or orientations of extraversion or introversion are associated with a function. In a sense, Jung continues the tradition of quaternary temperament even though he uses eight rather than four psychological types; but they are derived from four psychological functions.

Psychological Types was published in 1921 and later typologists such as Sheldon, Keirsey, and Myers-Briggs continue the Jungian line, developing various classifications based on the traditional idea of temperament, i.e., a set of emotional and behavioral predispositions, probably innate, that occur regularly and form an identifiable pattern. Temperament is that one aspect of personality that is biologically determined, although until now the mechanism of this determination has been unclear. What interests us most, however, is the concept of type, or some other equivalent, when associated with the concept of trait, as we shall see in the evolution of the so-called trait theories and their possible connections with the astrological analysis of temperament.

What is a Trait?

Psychologist Gordon Allport dedicated himself to the study of personality in its various aspects, representing it not only structurally but also, from the dynamic point of view, in terms of traits. The concept of trait occupies a central position in his theory and is defined as a "neuropsychic structure having the capacity to render many stimuli functionally equivalent, and to initiate and guide equivalent (meaningfully consistent) forms of adaptive and expressive behavior." (Allport, G.W., 1966.) In other words, the traits are somehow associated with the neurophysiologic structures that make up fundamental personality units. These orient behavior according to the perception of environmental stimuli, i.e., the meaning assigned to such stimuli. They can therefore operate in different environments and produce similar responses if similarities in meaning are perceived in seemingly disparate situations. Therefore, it is due to the equivalence of meanings that equivalent stimuli correspond to equivalent behaviors or responses. This he named functional equivalence, a fundamental concept to the understanding of what is discussed in the next chapter.

What is clear from this definition is that personality traits are associated with psychological interpretations and come into being as guides for responding to an external situational stimulus or set of stimuli, or even to an individual's internal state. It could be expressed as a behavioral algorithm, functioning as follows: if x is perceived, then act and/or feel in mode y. Of course this is a simplistic representation of psychological reality, but it serves to show that there are varying and reasonably stable ways of adapting to the environment that can be independent of learning. In fact, trait is the name given to a combination of certain kinds of behavior. Putting this in an equation:

$$T_1 = r_x + r_y + r_z \qquad T_2 = r_a + r_b + r_c \qquad T_3 + r_k + r_l + r_m$$

T_1, T_2 and T_3 are three given traits; for example, T_1 is Caution, T_2 is Altruism and T_3 is Aggressiveness. Each r belonging to a sum represents a certain behavior or habitual response. The three responses of each trait have a high probability of co-ocurrence, i.e., if the individual tends to act in the r_x way, it is very likely to also act in r_y an r_z. But what would that be like in practice, in terms of actual behavior? If the trait is T_1 (Caution), r_x could be "does not invest money in stocks," r_y could be "does not use a credit card on the Internet," and r_z could be "never trusts strangers." For T_2 (Altruism), r_a could be "gives alms to the poor," r_b could be "always helps relatives," and r_c "does volunteer work." For T_3 (Aggressiveness), r_k could be "often beats his children," r_l could be "if a subordinate commits an error, he starts swearing at him," and r_m could be "wants to smash the face of the driver who hit his car."

If we say someone is cautious, the person might be afraid of risky investments, might not make purchases online with a credit card, and might be wary of those they do not know. If one is seen as an altruistic person, he or she almost certainly will not hesitate to give alms to the poor, will not fail a relative in need, and will gladly do volunteer work. Similarly, an aggressive person has no patience with the pranks of children or with the mistakes of an employee and will be quick to anger when someone inadvertently cuts him off on the road. These are expected behaviors associated with a personality trait, which can be defined as inferences made from behavior observation. They are constructs. Their expression occurs frequently and in various situations, but not all. They serve to identify individuals.

The traits should persist more or less throughout a lifetime, at least from the beginning of adulthood. Furthermore, their identification requires observation in various contexts and situations. Only then can we go beyond the specific influences of every social situation, with the manipulations and controls that belong to them, and capture the underlying individual orientation to socially conditioned expressions and behavior. Social environments impose rules and standards of conduct on individuals. To be accepted, people should incorporate these indicators in their behavior; otherwise they will have great difficulty in adapting to these environments. This obviously creates a uniformity that inhibits conduct that goes against what is permissible and desirable. Without systematic observation that aggregates the many and varied behavioral responses of an individual in a wide spectrum of situations, we cannot perceive and infer the conceptual reality of the trait. Isolated acts do not tell us anything about a person, nor serve to predict what they will do when faced with other stimuli. To get to the trait, we must therefore add a large number of specific activities.

Before Allport, the concept of personality trait had already provided information for a quantitative study. Eysenck and Eysenck (1985) tell us that in the beginning of the last century (1909) G. Heymans and E. Wiersma, two Dutch psychologists, developed statistical correlational studies on traits. They also mention the work of Edward Webb (1915), who would have been the first to use the method of factor analysis to this end, followed by Garnett (1918), Thurstone (1934), McCloy (1936), Guilford (1936), and Reyburn and Taylor (1939). But the one who stood out in the investigation of quantitative traits using factor analysis was English psychologist Raymond Cattell. However, before discussing Cattell we must clarify the meaning of factor analysis and its importance in many modern trait theories.

Factor analysis is a statistical technique that seeks to discover correlations in a large number of variables. This method greatly simplifies the work of the researcher who needs to handle a large amount of data. In the case of psychologists, such data might be answers to questionnaire items or tests, the result being a vast array of data with seemingly nothing in common showing the possibility for the emergence of patterns. When some of the variables being studied are grouped, factor analysis enables us to infer the underlying factors or dimensions. Personality traits are factors of this nature inferred from the co-variation of several items, i.e., behavior patterns or responses that are associated because they occur together: in most cases, individuals whose answer is a, also answer b and c. Therefore, the behaviors *a*, *b*, and *c* comprise a factor, dimension, or personality trait. One arrives at this conclusion by analyzing a large group of individuals in order to derive a common trait. These factors reveal latent structures of personality.

An exploratory factor analysis aims to infer more general concepts (the traits) that will be applied to the population as a whole. From this research a scale of measures is created that will then serve to measure the score of a person regarding a particular trait, dimension, or personality factor. The difference between the modern concept of personality dimension and the old concepts of psychological type is that in the latter individuals receive a label for the type to which they belong. They are one thing and not another. For example, he is always phlegmatic, but never sanguine, choleric, or melancholic. In the case of the dimensions, all vary in scale, i.e., one is more or less dominant, more or less conservative, more or less affectionate, to name some of the traits found by Cattell.

Raymond Cattell

With previous experience in clinical child psychology, Raymond Cattell stood out in experimental psychology using multifactor analysis to study a large number of variables and the simultaneous interrelations between them. This method is ideal when you want to investigate the behavior of individuals under normal environmental situations. The starting point that led Cattell to formulate his theory of traits was a survey done by Allport and Odbert in 1936, when they selected more than 17,000 English words that describe personality traits and psychological states. Of this total, 4,500 traits were reduced to just 171, by choosing one out of many synonyms and eliminating unusual words as well as metaphors. Working with these personality descriptors and applying factor analysis to questionnaires completed by several subjects, Cattell arrived at sixteen factors, or traits of origin, that roughly correspond to a multidimensional structure of personality.

The sixteen factors of Q data (questionnaire data) developed by Cattell are presented as pairs of semantic opposites or bipolar dimensions: reserved/warm; concrete-thinking/abstract-thinking; emotional stability/reactive emotionally; deferential/dominant; serious/cheerful; disregards rules/rule-conscious; shy/socially bold; utilitarian/sensitive; trusting/vigilant; practical/imaginative; forthright/shrewd; self-assured/apprehensive; traditional/open to change; group-oriented/self-reliant; tolerates disorder/perfectionistic; relaxed/tense. Depending on the score of the self-assessment questionnaire, the person is either in the middle range between the two extremes, or closer to one pole. For each trait there is variation along an axis representing the entire spectrum of that dimension or personality factor. Therefore, each individual has a position in each of these factors.

What we see here is the construction of a taxonomy based on common words of natural language that serve to describe personality traits. This approach is called lexical because it is based on language and its attempt to codify human behavior in certain lexical units that are almost always adjectives such as aggressive, shy, generous, and conservative. Despite criticism of the possibility for replication of the results obtained by Cattell, thanks to his work we have arrived at the five major personality factors that today constitute the number accepted by most of the psychologists working with trait theories. But before speaking of the Five Factor model, also known as the Big Five, I will introduce another major researcher in trait theories who cannot be overlooked in any discussion that involves the quantitative study of personality factors or traits.

Hans Eysenck

Eysenck's personality model, as well as Cattell's, is basically descriptive (taxonomic), although it also presents some information explaining the biological mechanisms that contribute to determining behavior and individual differences. Eysenck initially identified two broad dimensions of personality that he called **E**xtraversion/Introversion and **N**euroticism/Emotional Stability. He then added one more, **P**sychoticism/Impulse control, thus creating a model called PEN. Here again, factor analysis was used to process the data from tests and questionnaires. These three dimensions are at the top of a hierarchical organization of personality that encompasses four levels: 1) specific responses; 2) habitual responses; 3) traits; and 4) types.

Specific responses are any situational behavior an individual does in their response to environmental stimuli. A behavior like laughing loudly after hearing a joke is a specific response that in itself reveals nothing about the subject's personality. Walking away without saying anything after being provoked by a bully is another specific response that in the same way, when taken alone, does not say much about the temperament of the person. We know nothing about the circumstances under which these actions occurred, nothing about the social pressures involved. In the first case, this attitude does not mean that the individual is a lively and humorous subject. Maybe the joke was been told by a boss and the individual just pretended to laugh to please a superior. In the second case, the example seems to refer to a quiet person who does not like fights or arguments. But this may not be the correct explanation. Maybe the individual was accompanied by a child and chose to spare her from an unpleasant and potentially dangerous situation.

Habitual responses are, as the name implies, frequent and recurring behavior. Those who always burst into laughter when jokes are told are said to be spontaneous and merry. Those who almost never react to provocation and who avoid confrontation are seen as peaceful, calm, and controlled. And what about traits? What would they be in Eysenck's opinion? The trait emerges from habitual behavior that is a construct developed from the application of factor analysis to behavioral variables. The concept, similar to Cattell's because both used similar methods, shows some discrepancies in results.

Finally, the type or dimension results from a second application of factor analysis, this time fac-

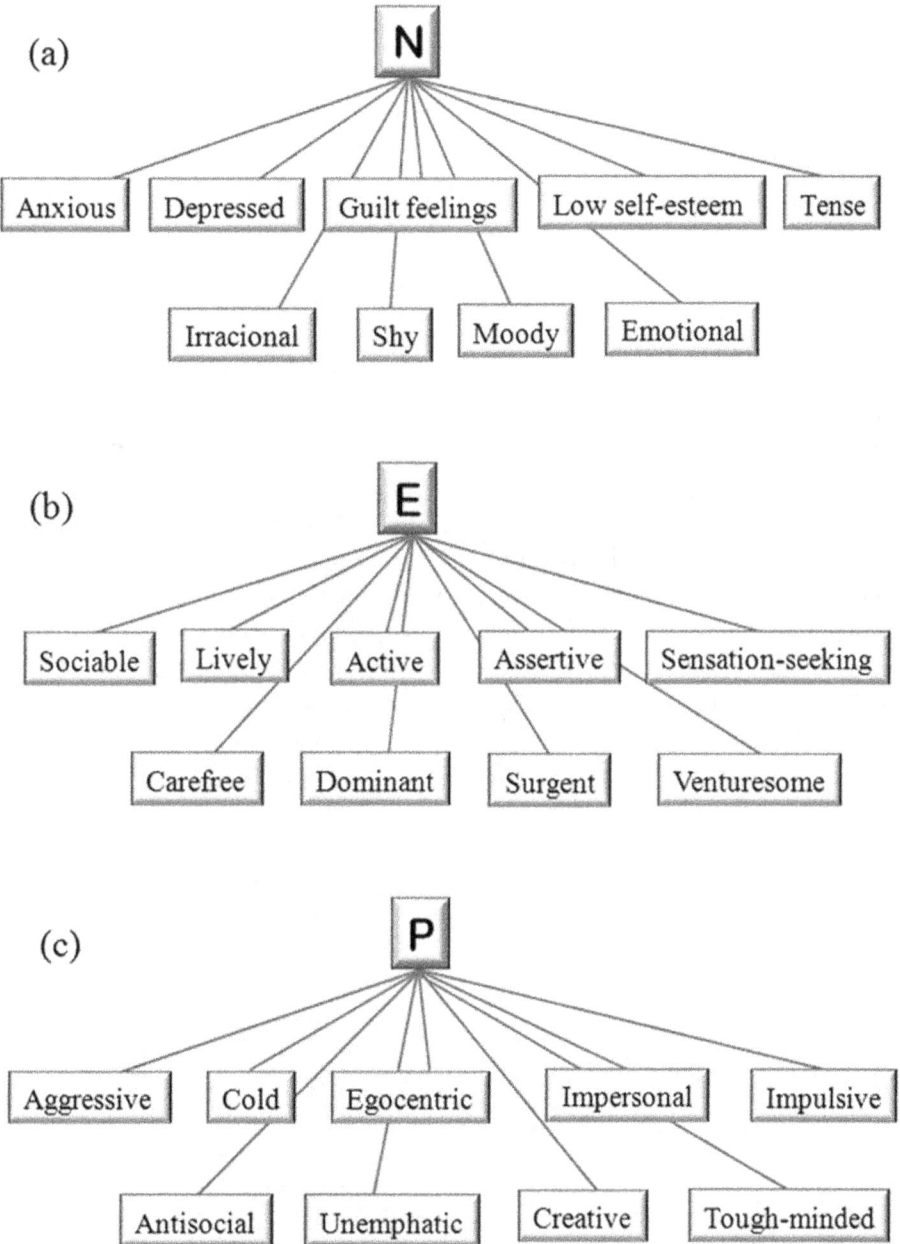

Figure 2.2 The Hierarchy of Personality Traits

toring or inter-correlating traits themselves to reach the three orthogonal super-factors. They are orthogonal because no further correlation is possible. For Eysenck, Extraversion, Neuroticism, and Psychoticism are the three fundamental dimensions of personality, at least with regard to the emotions. Here the traits correspond to Cattell's primary factors, and the types to his second order factors. Figure 2.2 shows three figures that depict Eysenck's hierarchical taxonomy with the factors that make up each dimension.

Eysenck recognized in his model that all of the theories of temperament converged, and these originated in the traditional doctrine of the four temperaments. The constituents of each temperament trait or psychological type are determined by genetic inheritance, while actual behavior, the actions and reactions of the subject in the real world, is socially and circumstantially influenced. We are therefore faced with a biosocial theory of personality that presents an explanation for the biological causes of individual differences. For each of the PEN dimensions, Eysenck attributed a neurophysiological mechanism that would justify, from a biological point of view, temperament orientations that are dissimilar.

Eysenck's model served as the basis for many other studies on the structural dimensions of personality and their possible physiological foundations, especially with regard to the Extraversion and Neuroticism dimensions, which he proposed, and that continue to appear, even with other names, in later works. Actually, not everything was confirmed. Biological explanations still seem far from satisfactory and the ternary structure was not confirmed; today the preference of most researchers is for a model of five factors, not three. Nevertheless, in Eysenck's descriptive system the emphasis on the interaction between biological and socio-cultural determinants and construction of verifiable hypotheses, which is not always the case in psychology, is a legacy of great importance to the advancement of research on human personality. Eysenck and Cattell made invaluable contributions to the quantification of individual differences and the influence of their work continues.

In view of this background, our dialogue between astrology and psychology will have as its specific target the current theories that propose a model of five factors. These alleged five dimensions of personality cover most human behavioral habits.

The Five Factors

This model proposes that there are five factors that cover a significant part of the structure of personality; it is dominant among the trait theories. Apparently there is little difference between the model of the Five Factors (FF) and Catttell's and Eysenck's model. Basically, they follow the same principles.

Applying factor analysis to a set of twenty-two variables used in a study of Cattell, Donald Fiske (1949) was the first to find a total of five factors. In the late 1950s, Tupes and Christal reviewed the data of Cattell and Fiske and also found five factors. In 1963, Norman reproduced these results and created a taxonomy for the five factors:

- I. Extraversion or Surgency
- II. Agreeableness
- III. Conscientiousness
- IV. Emotional Stability
- V. Culture.

The terms have not changed much since then. This same structure of the five factors was reproduced by Borgatta (1964) and Digman & Takemoto-Chock (1981).

But throughout the 1960s and 1970s there was not much interest in trait theories and personality measurements, a situation that was reversed in the mid-1980s with the work of Costa and McCrae, Goldberg, Digman, and others. That was when the FF model was created from the factor analysis of adjectives and personality descriptors of self-assessment questionnaires and evaluations made by observers. Moreover, cross-cultural studies, in their turn, have reinforced the universality of these five major personality dimensions.

The most important foundation of the FF model, called the lexical hypothesis, assumes that throughout evolution human beings linguistically encoded those aspects that are the most relevant features of personality, and consequently the behavior of the people to be assessed in social relations. These are precisely the aspects of personality traits that are then expressed in specific terms that overall permit the identification of individual differences. It was always important to make a prediction about how others would behave in various day-to-day situations.

The nomenclature of the five factors shows small variations from one author to another, implying not only differences in wording but also in content since some sub-factors or facets that are component traits of each of the five major factors (the Big Five, as they were called by Goldberg) belong to one factor or another, depending on the author. Costa and McCrae's classification and nomenclature, currently the most widely accepted taxonomy, are used in this book. Each factor is given a name that refers to only one of its poles. The dimensions of personality described by the model are a continuum that goes from one extreme to another, and most of the population is distributed in a normal curve, i.e., around the midpoint of these scales. Factors in the FF model of Costa and McCrae are:

- I. Extraversion
- II. Agreeableness
- III. Conscientiousness
- IV. Neuroticism
- V. Openness (to experience).

Extraversion and its polar opposite, Introversion, have been used since Jungian times, when they were still types. This dimension is one of the factors of the second order of Eysenck's model and is present in almost all existent trait theories, where it can appear under other names. It measures the frequency and intensity of interpersonal relations and activity level. It also serves to assess the need for variation in stimuli and the tendency of individuals to maintain a good mood or bad mood in their responses. The components (the facets) of this factor are *Warmth* (E_1), *Gregariousness* (E_2), *Assertiveness* (E_3), *Activity* (E_4), *Excitement-seeking* (E_5), and *Positive emotions* (E_6). Extraverts tend to be communicative, sociable, lively, enthusiastic, optimistic, and humorous. On the opposite side of the spectrum, introverts tend to be quiet, shy, placid, pessimistic, and sober. We all know that most people are not found at such extremes but hover around the midpoint and only occasionally behave like a typical extravert or introvert.

Agreeableness is the second factor and measures the degree of sympathy or antagonism in social relations, i.e., the tendency to cooperate or compete with peers. The facets are *Trust* (A_1), *Straightforwardness* (A_2), *Altruism* (A_3), *Compliance* (A_4), *Modesty* (A_5), and *Tender-mindedness* (A_6). People who excel in this factor tend to be generous, cooperative, kind, selfless, and understanding, while the opposite would be petty, competitive, rude, selfish, and cold. Remember that these are patterns of behavior; no one is friendly or rude all the time, and social roles greatly change the responses a subject gives. Note that in general the names of factors are words that relate to the more socially acceptable side of the scale. The exception, as we shall see, is Neuroticism.

Conscientiousness is a factor that corresponds to organizational ability and persistence in achieving goals. On the one side we have people who are organized, disciplined, responsible, dependable, and persevering. On the other are those who are disorganized, undisciplined, irresponsible, unreliable, and unmotivated. The components of this factor are *Competence* (C_1) *Order* (C_2), *Dutifulness* (C_3), *Achievement striving* (C_4), *Self-discipline* (C_5), and *Deliberation* (C_6). This is a very important factor, for example, in projecting performance in a professional activity requiring high levels of responsibility and discipline.

Neuroticism is used to evaluate the degree of emotional stability, anxiety, and propensity for certain psychological disorders. Its components are *Anxiety* (N_1), *Hostility* (N_2), *Depression* (N_3), *Self-consciousness* (N_4), *Impulsiveness* (N_5), and *Vulnerability* (N_6). People who score high in this factor tend to be tense, nervous, insecure, anxious, and unstable, while at the other end of the spectrum are those who are relaxed, calm, self-confident, carefree, and stable.

Finally, in **Openness**, interest in new experiences and the degree of tolerance for the unfamiliar and cultural breadth are assessed. It is a good indicator of creative potential. Its components are *Fantasy* (O_1), *Aesthetics* (O_2), *Feelings* (O_3), *Actions* (O_4), *Ideas* (O_5), and *Values* (O_6). These individuals are imaginative, original, daring, curious, and liberal, while those at the other end of the scale are conventional, fearful, restricted in their interests, and conservative.

The Facets

Each of the thirty facets is described here as a first step in articulating trait theories and psychological astrology, and in establishing a dialogue between different languages. The evaluation that assigns values to these factors covers, or tries to cover, the personality as a whole, or at least most of it. Astrology as I see it, on the other hand, covers temperament, or the biological nucleus of the personality.

Extraversion

Warmth (E_1): This indicates a tendency to be sociable and friendly, as well as ease in interpersonal relationships and making friends. Low scores indicate formal, distant, and reserved people.

Gregariousness (E_2): This indicates an enjoyment of the company of others; social contact is critical, and the individual has many friends. At the other end of the scale are the loners who do not seek stimuli of a social nature and do not like crowds.

Assertiveness (E_3): This individual has a strong personality and is dominant and influential, determined, and sure of himself or herself with leadership potential. When the score is low, the person prefers to stay in the background and is unassuming, modest, and withdrawn.

Activity (E_4): This indicates an accelerated rhythm of life, plenty of energy, and an individual who likes to keep busy and often engages in many activities. If the score is low, the person is sluggish and unhurried, and his or her pace is slow.

Excitement-seeking (E_5): This individual needs a variety of stimuli, enjoys bright colors and noisy environments, tends to take risks, and is easily bored. If the score is low, the subject is sober and cautious, tolerates routine, and does not like agitation.

Positive emotions (E_6): This individual tends to have a cheerful disposition, and is lively, optimistic, usually in a good mood, and often experiences feelings of happiness. At the other extreme the person is serious, serene, often pessimistic, and has little enthusiasm.

Agreeableness

Trust (A_1): This individual believes in others and is understanding and peaceful. At the opposite end of the scale is the individual who tends to be cynical, skeptical, and suspicious.

Straightforwardness (A_2): This individual tends to be sincere and open, is often naive, and puts his or her cards on the table. A low score is associated with shrewdness, cleverness, manipulation, flattery, and dissimulation.

Altruism (A_3): This indicates an individual who is concerned with others, empathic, caring and generous. At the opposite end of the scale is the individual who tends to be egocentric and selfish and does not get involved with other people's problems.

Compliance (A_4): This individual tends to be tolerant, forgiving, gentle, docile, respectful, and helpful, and avoids confrontation. Those with the lowest scores are inflexible, demanding, stubborn and insensitive.

Modesty (A_5): This indicates a discreet personality, unassuming and humble, but not necessarily because of low self-esteem. At the other end of the scale is the individual who is arrogant and presumptive and has an air of superiority.

Tender-mindedness (A_6): This individual is sentimental, generous, and benevolent, and cares for others. Those with a low score tend to have a "cold heart" and are cold, calculating, objective, and realistic.

Conscientiousness

Competence (C_1): This individual tends to be efficient, thorough, and sensible, and performance in objective tasks is generally very good. With low scores, the individual is often unprepared, inept, confused, and distracted.

Order (C_2): This person is organized, methodical, and careful, and follows routines and schedules. When the score is low, he or she can be messy, sloppy, careless, and chaotic.

Dutifulness (C_3): This individual has a tendency to fulfill obligations and to act with scruples, which makes him/her reliable and responsible; at the other extreme, he or she tends to be irresponsible.

Achievement striving (C_4): A high score corresponds to an individual with high levels of aspiration and ambition, and one who will work hard to achieve his or her goals. If the score is low, the tendency is to be unmotivated, carefree, or even lazy.

Self-discipline (C_5): This individual is persistent and finishes what he or she starts, strong-willed, self-controlled, and determined. Low scores indicate great difficulty performing long-term tasks, lack of determination and concentration, and a tendency to easily drop things.

Deliberation (C_6): This indicates an indivdual who is cautious, thoughtful, and prudent, and thinks and considers before making decisions or acting. At the opposite extreme, the person tends to be hurried, hasty, impulsive, and spontaneous, and often makes decisions without thinking.

Neuroticism

Anxiety (N_1): Individuals with high scores are tense, nervous, anxious, fearful, and uneasy. On the other hand, low scores indicate calm, quiet, carefree people.

Hostility (N_2): This individual tends to often feel anger, bitterness, resentment, and frustration. At the other end of the scale, the individual is friendly, balanced, and gentle.

Depression (N_3): This indicates an indivdual who often has feelings of sadness, loneliness, guilt, hopelessness, and unhappiness. A low score indicates that it is rare for the individual to feel depressed or anxious.

Self-consciousness (N_4): This person often feels ashamed and embarrassed in social situations, and feelings of ridicule and inferiority also tend to be common. At the other end of the scale, the individual is self-assured, confident, and feels comfortable in public.

Impulsiveness (N_5): This individual has great difficulty controlling desires, emotional impulses, and temptations in general, and his or her sense of gratification must be immediate. With a low score, the person has moderate self-control and can wait for gratification.

Vulnerability (N6): This individual has difficulty coping with stress, experiences feelings of panic in emergency situations, and has a high sensitivity to stimuli. If the score is low, he or she tends to be tough, almost undisturbed by adverse conditions, and cold-blooded when faced with danger.

Openness

Fantasy (O_1): This person has a fertile imagination with a tendency to daydream and explore his or her inner world and creativity, along with having his or her head in the clouds. On the opposite side, the individual is pragmatic and realistic, and has his or her feet on the ground.

Aesthetics (O_2): The individual appreciates art, has a heightened sensitivity to various artistic expressions, and greatly values the aesthetic experience. On the other hand, the individual with a low score, has little interest in or is indifferent to aesthetic values and has difficulty understanding artistic vision.

Feelings (O_3): This indidvidual values the emotions and is very sensitive and empathetic. On the other hand, a low score indicates insensitivity and rather limited emotional experience.

Actions (O_4): This indicates an indivdual who is always looking for new experiences, does not tolerate routine, has a sense of adventure, and needs a wide variety of stimuli. If the score is low, he or she tends to be resistant to change, prefers what is familiar and is not bothered by routine.

Ideas (O_5): This person has an intellectual curiosity for new ideas and a willingness to explore unconventional views, and is open-minded and attracted to philosophical questions. At the other end of the scale, the person is pragmatic, does not question established ideas, and his or her interests are limited to only a few issues.

Values (O_6): This indicates an individual who is tolerant and liberal, questions truths, and considers new values, whether social, political or religious. The opposite individual is conservative, dogmatic, and conformist.

Factors, Facets and Cosmosigns

This is a first attempt to establish correlations between the factors and their facets and the semantic content of the astrological signs, or cosmosigns. The relationships presented here are purely empirical, and the goal is to be able to provide guidance for a more elaborate and controlled study. The purely astrological meanings used here differ somewhat from those assigned to the cosmosigns by say conventional astrology, but nothing that will cause much surprise to those who have some knowledge of astrology. For more details on the construction of these meanings, see Chapter 3. The correspondence between astrological sign and facet means that the traits, or most of the traits that make up the sub-factor, are part of the semantic field of the cosmosign.

Extraversion (E)

This factor corresponds mainly to traits associated with the fire signs–Aries, Leo, and Sagittarius– and the air signs–Gemini, Libra, and Aquarius.

E_1, *warmth*: Aries, Gemini, Cancer, Leo, Libra, Sagittarius

E_2, *gregariousness*: Aries, Gemini, Leo, Libra, Sagittarius

E_3, *assertiveness*: Aries, Leo, Sagittarius

E_4, *activity*: Aries, Gemini, Sagittarius, Aquarius

E_5, *excitement-seeking*: Aries, Gemini, Leo, Sagittarius, Aquarius

E_6, *positive emotions*: Aries, Gemini, Leo, Sagittarius

Agreeableness (A)

This factor is strongly associated with Cancer and Pisces (water), partly with the three fire signs, and with Virgo (earth) and Libra (air). Unlike the Extraversion factor, it includes cosmosigns of all the elements, although more emphatically of the water element.

A_1, *trust*: Cancer, Libra, Sagittarius, Pisces

A_2, *straightforwardness*: Aries, Cancer, Leo, Sagittarius

A_3, *altruism*: Cancer, Virgo, Libra, Pisces

A_4, *compliance*: Cancer, Libra, Pisces

A_5, *modesty*: Cancer, Virgo, Pisces

A_6, *tender-mindedness*: Cancer, Pisces

Conscientousness (C)

This factor is identified almost entirely with the cosmosigns of the earth element. But it also appears in signs of other elements: Scorpio (water), Aquarius (air), and Leo (fire).

C_1, *competence*: Taurus, Virgo, Scorpio, Capricorn, Aquarius

C_2, *order*: Taurus, Virgo, Scorpio, Capricorn

C_3, *dutifulness*: Leo, Virgo, Capricorn

C_4, *achievement striving*: Leo, Virgo, Scorpio, Capricorn, Aquarius

C_5, *self-discipline*: Taurus, Leo, Virgo, Scorpio, Capricorn

C_6, *deliberation*: Taurus, Virgo, Scorpio, Capricorn

Neuroticism (N)

This factor is more often associated with water signs: Cancer, Scorpio, and Pisces. But it also appears with some strength in Virgo (earth), Capricorn (earth), and Aries (fire), and with less emphasis in Sagittarius (fire), Gemini (air), and Aquarius (air).

N_1, *anxiety*: Aries, Gemini, Virgo, Scorpio, Capricorn, Aquarius

N_2, *hostility*: Aries, Scorpio

N_3, *depression*: Cancer, Virgo, Scorpio, Capricorn, Pisces

N_4, *self-consciousness*: Virgo, Capricorn

N_5, *impulsiveness*: Aries, Cancer, Sagittarius, Pisces

N_6, *vulnerability*: Cancer, Pisces

Openness (O)

This factor shows a strong correspondence with the air and fire cosmosigns, especially Aquarius and Gemini (air), and Sagittarius (fire), followed by a reasonable expression in Cancer (water) and Pisces (water). Its expression in the earth element is limited to Taurus.

O_1, *fantasy*: Aries, Cancer, Sagittarius, Aquarius, Pisces

O_2, *aesthetics*: Taurus, Cancer, Leo, Libra, Pisces

O_3, *feelings*: Cancer, Pisces

O_4, *actions*: Aries, Gemini, Sagittarius, Aquarius

O_5, *ideas*: Gemini, Sagittarius, Aquarius

O_6, *values*: Gemini, Libra, Sagittarius, Aquarius

These correspondences not only facilitate the use of common expressions between personality psychology and astrology but also the construction of algorithms that can be used to translate the reading of the astrological chart in terms of the Five Factors model (or similar models). In addition, we begin to work with operational concepts, fundamental for experimental work and validation, and not with vague metaphysical ideas. Of course as soon as these assumptions are tested there will be alterations, a normal part of scientific research. This is a first approach and purely empirical, but it is a step toward abandoning the obscure language of Jungian psychology and or, still worse, the astrological language of bygone ages.

Cloninger's model: Dimensions of Temperament

According to the theory of psychiatrist C. Robert Cloninger, the dimensions of temperament are actually part of a larger model that includes seven factors. Four of them are dimensions of temperament and the other three are dimensions of character. Environmental influences determine the dimensions of character, while the dimensions of temperament are determined by biological factors.

At first Cloninger built a psychobiological model in which temperament had three dimensions: Novelty Seeking (NS), Harm Avoidance (HA) and Reward Dependence (RD). Later he added another one, Persistence (P), formerly a component of RD.

The Cloninger model is mentioned here because it is widely used in studies on the biological determinants of personality. In Chapter 4, Biological Foundations, we shall see some neurochemical details of this model. For now, we'll use a brief description of each of these dimensions and their relation to the five factors according to the correlation analysis performed by De Fruyt *et al* (2000).

Novelty Seeking (NS): Individuals who score high in NS are impulsive, inquisitive, easily excitable, easily irritated, volatile, extravagant, and unruly. They seek new activities but tend to quickly lose interest. In relationships, they are inconsistent and unstable. Those with low scores are not very enthusiastic and not very keen to seek new activities, worry about details, think for a long time before making their decisions, and are reflexive, rigid, loyal and systematic. Regarding the model of the Five Factors, the NS factor correlates positively with the factors Extraversion and Openness, and negatively with Conscientiousness.

Harm Avoidance (HA): High scores in HA correspond to people who are cautious, tense, apprehensive, inhibited, and shy, and who tire easily. On the other hand, individuals with low scores are confident, optimistic, carefree, uninhibited and energetic. Factor HA correlates positively with Neuroticism and negatively with Extraversion.

Reward Dependence (RD): High RD scores characterize helpful, compassionate, sentimental, sensitive, affectionate and impressionable individuals. On the other hand, low scores indicate socially indifferent, emotionally cold, pragmatic, and objective people. The RD factor correlates mainly with Agreeableness and secondarily with Openness.

Persistence (P): People who attain above average scores on P are industrious, hardworking, persistent, ambitious, perfectionistic, and are resistant to frustration and fatigue. In contrast, those whose scores are low are indolent, unstable, and distracted, have low initiative when faced by obstacles, and easily give up. The P factor is correlated with the Conscientiousness dimension.

Astrological Circumplex?

The first circular representation of the personality was created by astrologers in the form of an astrological chart, which contains components that comprise a network of intertwined and dynamically ordered meanings. This invaluable contribution of astrology to the understanding of human personality, although disdained by mainstream science, was used in part, whether consciously or unconsciously, by psychologists who sought an appropriate way to portray and evaluate interpersonal behavior. The circular model of the interpersonal system is based mainly on the studies of psychiatrist Harry Stack Sullivan, psychoanalyst Erik Erikson, and in group psychotherapy sessions conducted by Freedman, Timothy Leary, Ossorio, and Coffey in the early 1950s. It was later called the interpersonal circumplex, a reference to the concept created by Louis Guttman in 1954, which defined circumplex as a circular system for the ordering of variables.

Table 2.2 Domains, Facets, Dimensions of Temperament and Cosmosigns			
Domain	Facets	Dimensions of Temperament	Cosmosigns
Extraversion	Warmth (E_1)		Aries
	Gregariousness (E_2)	Positive: Novelty Seeking	Gemini
	Assertiveness (E_3)	Negative: Harm Avoidance	Leo
	Ativity (E_4)		Sagittarius
	Excitement-seeking (E_5)		
	Positive emotions (E_6)		
Agreeableness	Trust (A_1)		Cancer
	Straighrforwardness (A_2)	Positive: Reward Dependence	Libra
	Altruism (A_3)		Pisces
	Compliance (A_4)		
	Modesty (A_5)		
	Tender-mindedness (A_6)		
Conscientiousness	Competence (C_1)		Taurus
	Order (C_2)	Negative: Novelty-seeking	Leo
	Dutifulness (C_3)	Positive: Persistence	Virgo
	Achievement striving (C_4)		Scorpio
	Self-discipline (C_5)		Capricorn
	Deliberation (C_6)		
Neuroticism	Anxiety (N_1)		Aries
	Hostility (N_2)	Positive: Harm Avoidance	Cancer
	Depression (N_3)		Virgo
	Self-consciousness (N_4)		Scorpio
	Impulsiveness (N_5)		Capricorn
	Vulnerability (N_6)		Pisces
Openness	Fantasy (O_1)		Gemini
	Aesthesics (O_2)	Positive: Novelty seeking	Cancer
	Feelings (O_3)	Negative: Reward Dependence	Sagittarius
	Actions (O_4)		Aquarius
	Ideas (O_5)		Pisces
	Values (O_6)		

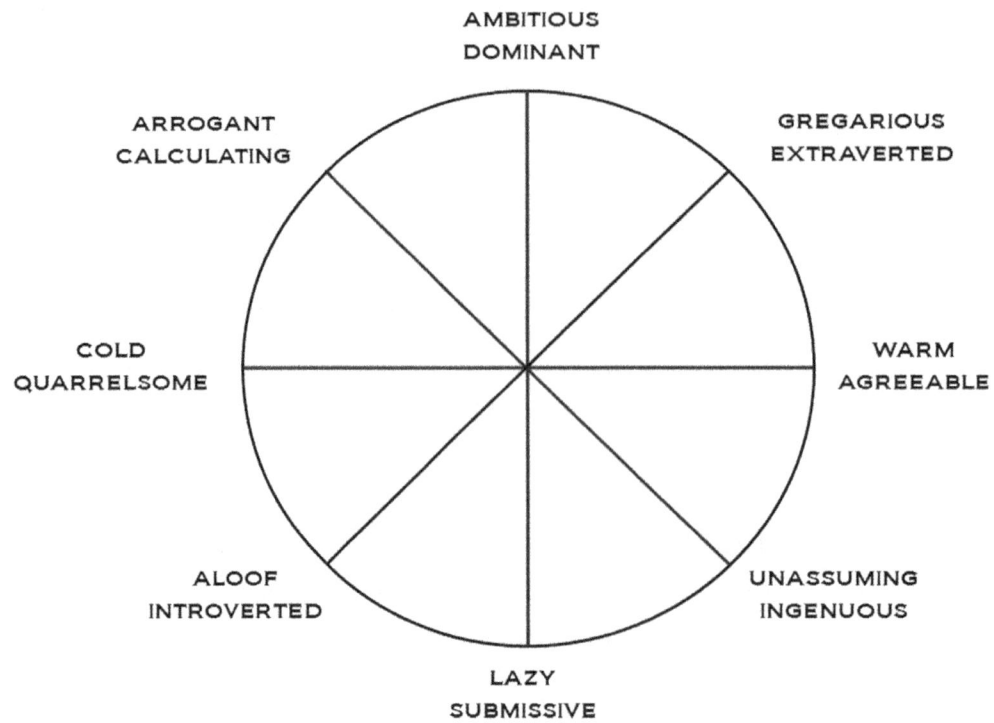

Figure 2.3 Interpersonal Circumplex with Eight Variables

This structural and correlational model of interpersonal behavior may, depending on the version, cover eight or sixteen variables divided into interpersonal categories along two orthogonal axes: the axis of control (vertical) and the axes of affiliation (horizontal), which represent the dimensions of dominance-submission and affiliation-hostility, respectively. Similar variables are found closer in the circle, variables opposite of each other are 180 degrees apart, and unrelated variables are separated by a distance of 90 degrees. The objective is to evaluate interpersonal traits on a scale. Figure 2.3 is an example of a diagram with eight interpersonal variables, each occupying an octant, i.e., one of eight divisions of the circle.

The two orthogonal axes and the four nodal points–dominance-submission and affiliation-hostility–generate, by combination, the other factors in the picture. This arrangement entails certain systematic relations between the points/factors that depend on their position in the circle. Thus each one is defined by its distance relationship with the others, not unlike the relationship between the zodiacal signs. Structurally, the logic is the same.

In astrology it is also possible to establish relationships of greater or lesser similarity according to angular distance. If the distance between the signs is 120 degrees (trine), which equates to four seg-

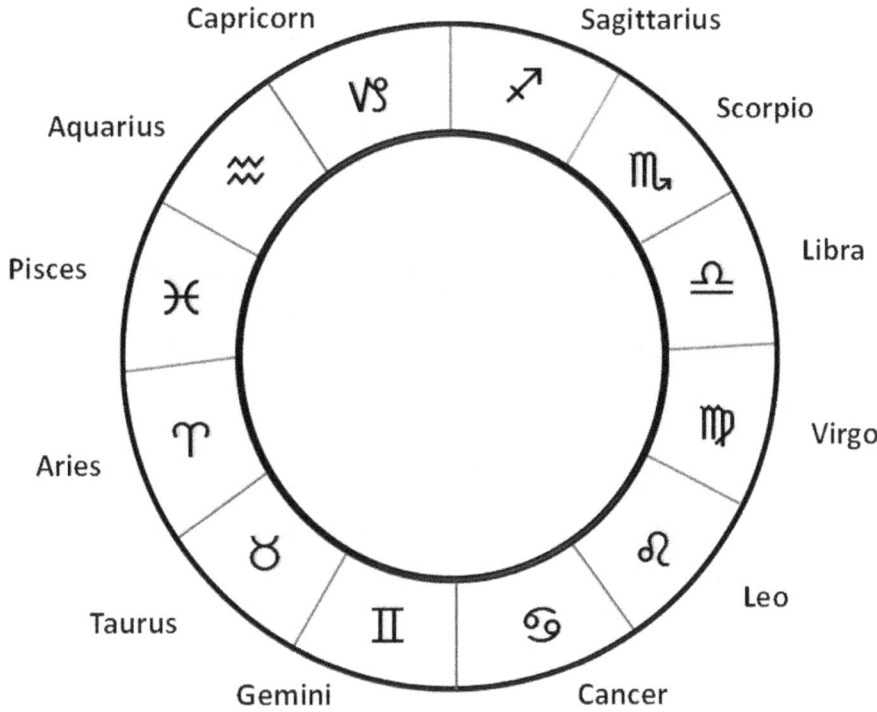

Figure 2.4 The Natural Sequence of the Zodiac Signs

ments of 30 degrees (four signs), it is said that the signs belong to the same element and therefore their semantic fields have many similarities. If the distance is 60 degrees (sextile), or two segments (two signs), there are a certain number of points in common that make them fairly compatible; this occurs between the elements fire and air, and earth and water. If the signs are opposite–a distance of 180 degrees (opposition) or six segments (six signs)–they can either clash with or complement each other; the opposing elements are fire and air, and earth and water. The relationships of dissimilarity are shown in angular distances of 30 (semi-sextile, one sign) and 90 degrees (square, or three signs); these always involve incompatible signs: fire or air, or earth or water. The ordering or relationship is therefore different from that established in the circumplex. In the zodiacal circle, adjacent dodecants (each segment of 30 degrees) represent a high degree of dissimilarity. The structural logic, however, remains the same.

Following the sequence of the zodiac signs in Figure 2.4, the circle begins with Aries, which has greater resonance with cosmosigns located at 120 degrees from it, or Leo and Sagittarius. Aries resonates less with Gemini and Aquarius, at 60 degrees, and Libra, the opposite cosmosign, at 180 degrees. Dissonance is expressed by Cancer and Capricorn, both at 90 degrees, and Taurus and

Pisces at 30 degrees. Each of these cosmosigns differs from Aries in certain specific aspects. A more detailed analysis would indicate that contiguous cosmosigns seem to be as (or more) dissimilar to each other as signs that are 90 degrees apart.

These relationships are essential in interpretation, facilitating the understanding of the meanings of each cosmosign according to its position in the zodiacal circle. Working in this sense, the astrologer can objectively and precisely describe the dynamics of the person's temperament. The astrologer can then inform the client about relationships, career, job family, finance, etc. However, the chart is not a crystal ball, nor is it, in my opinion, a basis for psychoanalysis or even to identify the individual's supposed mission on Earth. The temperament (and personality) of any human being has many contradictions and inconsistencies. The astrologer sees the full complexity of this reality represented symbolically in the natal chart, and his or her role is to inform the client of this psychological reality and its possible relationship with the outside world.

The descriptors used to characterize personality traits are therefore critical. Unfortunately, when learning astrology, some students study Greek mythology in order to grasp the meaning of both the signs and planets. This is not a waste of time, but using only mythology to create a conceptual framework can lead to unsatisfactory and misleading results. Too often astrologers reject science in favor of an emphasis on Jungian theories.

Three

Introduction to Minimalist Astrology

In order to clarify my proposal for scientific astrology, some fundamental astrological concepts that have been neglected, or that are incompletley defined, require more explanation. An objective and useful description is necessary in order to faciliate transparency and communication among astrologers, something that is especially important if we want to validate this system of knowledge and integrate it with the other sciences. The concepts of sign, language, grammar, syntax, and semantics all need to be defined.

Signs and Semiotics

The word "sign" is widely used in astrology, and people commonly ask "what's your sign," referring to the position in the zodiac of the Sun on the birth date. This is the best known part of astrology. Unfortunately, the horoscopes that appear online and in newspapers and popular magazines are confused with "legitimate" astrology but pale in comparison to an astrological consultation based on an accurate, timed birth chart. The word sign is associated more with astrology than any other area of knowledge; however, the word is a generic term that identifies the units of different semiotic systems. Let's look at some definitions.

Linguist Émile Benveniste said, "The role of the sign is to represent, to take the place of something else evoking it as a substitute." In its simplest and more universal definition, a sign is something that represents something else. It can be viewed from two perspectives and linked to the two main sign theories: semiotic structuralism as presented by Swiss linguist Ferdinand de Saussure, and the semiotics of American philosopher Charles S. Peirce. For the former, the sign is dyadic and he disregards the referent, i.e., the object represented; its expression and content is of a conceptual nature. For Peirce, however, a sign is triadic and takes into account the thing represented by the sign, i.e., the object it designates. Peirce's semiotics relate to the natural sciences and studies on cognition and artificial intelligence, while structuralist semiotics work better with the concept of verbal language, especially when it involves linguistic signs.

Celestial bodies are natural entities that transit the environment and their objective behavior is of course of interest. Agent and environment somehow interfere indirectly with human life, which points to triadic semiotics. However, the sophisticated language of the dynamics of astrological symbols in a chart demands an analysis of structure, where the meaning of each indicator and each element of the system is defined not only by itself but in its relationship with the others. Here we need linguistic tools, or perhaps more correctly, the semiotics of Peirce potentially contain structuralist semiotics.

According to Peirce, the sign can relate to its object in three ways. In each one, it receives a specific name: icon, index, and symbol. The icon or iconic sign establishes with the object a relationship of resemblance or similarity in an attempt to be identical to the thing being represented. Examples of icons are the landmark miniatures sold as souvenirs, a landscape drawn on a sheet of paper, a diagram, and even a metaphor. The index or indexical sign presents a dynamic and effective relationship with its object, establishing a real correspondence, as is the case of a link of contiguity, inclusion, or cause and effect. A clock, a road sign, any measuring instrument, the footprint of an animal, a cry of pain, and dark clouds in the sky are all examples of indexical signs. The last three can also be called natural signs because they are not artificial or created or shaped by human culture. This is of particular interest for us. The footprints show that a specific living thing passed through an area; the cry, depending on its characteristics, refers to something other than itself, i.e., pain, joy, or fear; and dark clouds often precede rain, meaning that water will fall from the sky. Therefore, footsteps, crying, and clouds act as signs of an animal, a pain, and rain, respectively.

The symbol is a sign that always presupposes a social convention. It is social because it is elaborated and used within a community or group of individuals for whom it makes sense. The symbol, which bears no resemblance or direct link with the object it represents, therefore depends on rules and has the ability to generate multiple meanings, successively unfolding until infinity. As Charles Peirce said, "the symbols grow." The only biological entity capable of generating and interpreting symbolic signs is the human being, designated therefore as a symbolic animal. The most sophisticated and developed system of symbols used by our species are natural languages, the unique universal language of all human societies, without exception. Linguistic signs are so versatile that they can be used to express any kind of language, be it graphical-visual, gesture, or sound. When an astrologer reads a chart, he or she translates or decodes the symbolic language of astrology into words. Astrology therefore operates a symbolic language by using all the characters that we saw in Chapter 2 to generate meanings. Its references are the planets of the solar system, the Sun, the Moon, some virtual points and segments in space, and some angular distances between celestial bodies.

The first manifestations of an astromancy ocurred in Babylon. *Baru* priests interpreted as signs of the gods a whole range of natural signs that ranged from the entrails of a sheep to the movement of the stars. These supposed signs were interpreted as coded messages or replies from the gods in anticipation of a future event. As such, the planets, as natural entities seen in the sky, were simply natural indexical signs of something, or even of an event, when occupying a particular sector of space, this also being an index with its own meaning. They were not symbols because they had not been produced by human culture, but became a symbolic sign when they received a name (linguistic sign) so as to be a concept that then was part of a system of beliefs. Here, the main thing to understand is that the symbols are always culturally generated; they never appear spontaneously. On the other hand, biological entities, including humans, are creatures "programmed" phylogenetically to recognize, interpret, and respond to some natural indexical signs, and their survival depends on it.

We call *semiosis* the process by which the sign, whatever it is, in some way represents an object or referent–that is, something else that is not itself–to a interpretant system, which can be either a living thing, human or animal, or any other natural or artificial system. *Semiotics* is the discipline that studies the phenomenon of significance. Therefore, the zodiac, which is the grand stage of astrological meanings, can be defined as a *semiotic circle* in which all semiotic dynamics of signs are organized to create meanings associating celestial mechanics, including other things, to the structure of the human personality or temperament. Each of the symbols that appear there–for example, a zodiac sign–unfolds in a broad range of consistent meanings, forming a *semantic field*; that is, a field of correlated meanings. The zodiac signs can be seen, from a psychological point of view, as behavior categories. Experience suggests that the astrological chart behaves like a topological representation of the different personality structures, or better still, of the temperament, and their dynamic relationships over time.

The Cosmosign

To better describe the astrological correlations, think of the zodiac as a circular astronomical space that generates meanings articulated by the personality, or by some of its levels or structures. The reading of this sign system tells us how an individual born at a given time and at a given geographic location tends to mentally represent the reality and act according to this representation (but not only according to it), forming regular patterns or habits of response or behavior. When interpreting the correlational phenomenon that links the celestial mechanics with the human personality, the zodiac signs, or cosmosigns, emerge.

Each zodiac sign, or cosmosign, is composed of a field of meanings, correlated and coherent among themselves. The astrological sign, therefore, is seen as a semantic field which by virtue of its meaning, guides and conditions the perception and the human interpretation of physical, psychological and social realities. This guidance, this necessary perceptual bias, corresponds to a combination of several traits observed in human behavior: how people respond to opportunities, challenges and threats from the environment, and how they interpret that environment. Habitual attitudes form an identifiable pattern of behavior that can be categorized according to the characteristics observed.

The perceptual selectivity in humans probably results from both genetic factors and socio-cultural conditioning. We do not know, however, how the astrological phenomenon is linked and interacts with these other factors. Empirical observation of the correlations between celestial mechanics and human personalities, although not exactly scientific, allowed the construction of a model to interpret the dynamics of these correlations. This model is the astrological chart, whose complexity in principle seems quite appropriate for a psychological analysis. Of course this is not a finished model but one that can and should be submitted to criticism. It is precisely this traditional model which in part will be questioned here and for which proposals will be presented for conceptual changes. The intention is to describe the astrological phenomenon in another way, or better still, from another perspective that I believe will make much more sense to contemporary minds. This new description will facilitate the understanding of this correlational phenomenon, will allow a more intelligent reading of the astrological chart, will eliminate the many mistakes made in the past and, finally, make this system of knowledge easier to verify, validate and refute (falsify).

In this theoretical framework the psychological concept of cosmosign is produced from personality traits correlated with each other, as already seen in the case of the inference of factors or dimensions of personality. In the same manner, personality traits are inferred from specific behaviors that characterize them. For example, aggression is a trait that can be seen in specific behaviors such as imposing one's opinion by force; reacting to a slight provocative stimulus with great emotion and yelling; reacting to offenses or alleged offenses with punches and kicks; educating children by beating them; and so on. Another personality trait is competitiveness: always wanting to be the winner; making a great effort to show that you are the best at what you do; being devastated when you lose a fight; having a strong desire to experience confrontation and to participate in competitions, etc.

Both aggression and competitiveness are traits found with higher intensity in the Aries cosmosign, the first of the zodiac. These personality traits can be called signical traits, and therefore a cosmosign is a unique set of signical traits that defines and makes it different from other cosmosigns. Other traits that could define Aries are a strong desire for social acceptance, self-centeredness, courage, dynamism, excitability, etc.

The Taurus cosmosign, which is the second of the zodiac, shows quite different signical characteristics than its neighbor Aries: a strong need for security, stubbornness, strong resistance to change, pragmatism, possessiveness, sensuality, among others. The third sign, Gemini, shows the following characteristics: flexibility, a good articulation of ideas, perceptiveness, communication, inquisitiveness, sense of humor, indecision, etc. And so on, until we get to Pisces, which completes the zodiacal circle and precedes Aires. Obviously it would be naive to think that a person's behavior reflects the dynamics of the astrological chart, and that this reflex, properly coded, can be decoded competently when reading the chart, as if we could see a whole psychological reality unfolding before our eyes. Surely this is not what happens. It is important to emphasize that, fundamentally, human behavior is a function of personality and the stimulus situation that the individual encounters. (Personality, we know, is determined by both genetic and socio-cultural factors.) One cannot fail to take into account, on the one hand, the demands of different social roles, and, on the other, the reaction to specific situations. *The stronger the pressure of social norms and obligations, the less evident are the personality traits that make up the person's own pattern, and the same is true of the correlation between the astrological chart and the individual's behavior.*

You do not see, therefore, the real personality in the astrological chart, but the potential personality, with its parameters for behavior orientation and the resulting preferred responses. We can also call this potential personality the temperament and imagine it as a nucleus from which the real personality is formed. Wanting to see beyond this core, astrologers of Jungian inspiration project onto the chart meanings that it does not hold and, worse, try to guess a whole life story, with its possible traumas, conflicts with parental figures, repression, or other factors that are situations dependent on unpredictable external factors and very probably not predictable by astrology. It is true that in astrological practice, especially when using forecasting techniques, everything seems to show that the chart refers to external reality and therefore implies the dynamic design of an entire network of interpersonal and institutional relationships.

Semantic Axes

In Figure 3.1 (see page 42), each pair of opposite cosmosigns in the zodiac forms a semantic axis represented by a double arrow. Linguist and semiotician A. J. Greimas defines semantic axis as the common denominator of two terms in opposition. The relationship of opposition between the two meanings of cosmosigns 180 degrees apart assumes a domain whose scope contains two fundamental and complementary poles. In my psychological approach to the zodiac, I shall first identify the axial signical traits as guidelines and also as prevailing and characteristic orientations and desires, and then later describe the specific field of each cosmosign with keywords.

Axis 1-7, Aries-Libra, Desire for Acceptance

Aries: search for acceptance by imposition. Keywords: self-assertion; domination; competition; aggressiveness; courage; leadership; intense activity; energy; physicality; self-centeredness; excitability; extraversion; impatience; impulsiveness; changeability; initiative; instability; constant motion; rashness.

Libra: search for acceptance by compromise. Keywords: sociability; conciliation; accommodation; agreement; friendliness; cooperation; persuasion; diplomacy; negotiation; harmonization; peacemaking; tolerance; symmetry; balance; fairness; moderation; flexibility; cordiality; politeness; delicacy; refinement; aesthetics; indecision; uncertainty.

Axis 2-8, Taurus-Scorpio, Desire for Security and Permanence

Taurus: seeking security through the accumulation of material goods. Keywords: attachment; retention; greed; possessiveness; jealousy; materialism; pragmatism; realism; stability; belief; inflexibility; caution; thrift; persistence; perseverance; endurance; patience; obstinacy; slowness; tranquility; sensuality.

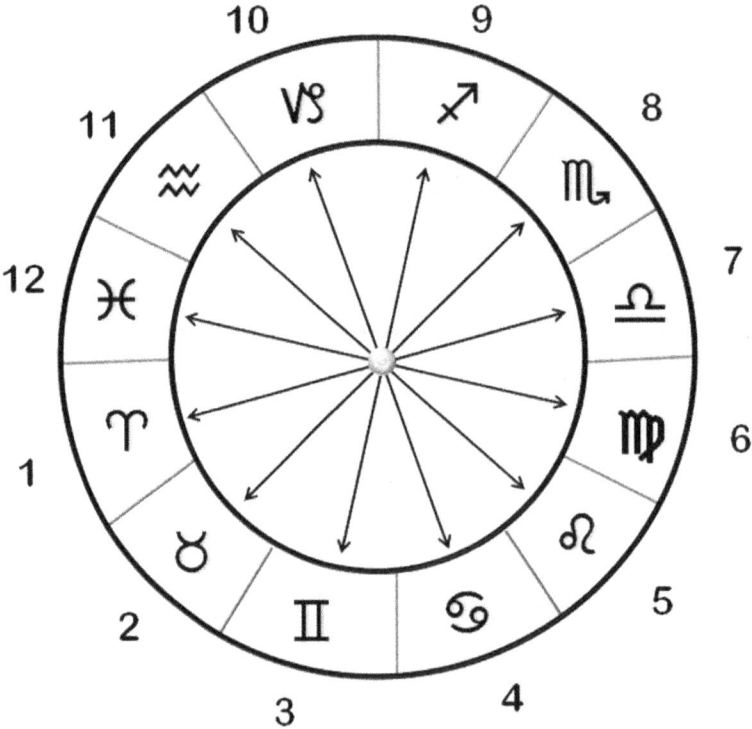

Figure 3.1 The Axes of the Zodiac Circle

Scorpio: seeking security by control of the situation. Keywords: manipulation; strategy; perceptiveness; shrewdness; introspection; determination; resistance; resilience; tenacity; persistence; radicalism; distrust; pessimism; concealment; austerity; rigidity; obsession; passion.

Axis 3-9, Gemini-Sagittarius, Desire for Multiple Stimuli

Gemini: search for stimulus from information. Keywords: variety; multiplicity; agitation; versatility; adaptation; flexibility; word skill; communication; talkativeness; discursiveness; inconstancy; indecision; instability; shrewdness; agility; fluency; irony; playfulness; humor.

Sagittarius: search for stimulus from adventure. Keywords: exploration; extraversion; diversity; volubility; liberality; prodigality; exaggeration; extravagance; freedom; anarchy; dissipation; daring; irreverence; euphoria; animation; joy; self-confidence; sincerity; optimism; hedonism.

Axis 4-10, Cancer-Capricorn, Desire for Commitment and Bonding (Conservation)

Cancer: search for bonding through emotion. Keywords: affection; sentimentality; hospitality; warmth; affability; nostalgia; preservation; tradition; family; imagination; protection; emotional security.

Capricorn: search for commitment through social responsibility. Keywords: restraint; conformity; constancy; discipline; discretion; stability; firmness; introversion; organization; permanence; pessimism; prudence; modesty; rigidity; seriousness.

Axis 5-11, Leo-Aquarius, Desire for Visibility and Distinction

Leo: search for visibility through self-expression. Keywords: self-esteem; authority; pride; honor; vanity; pomposity; ostentation; arrogance; creativity; fun; generosity; sophistication.

Aquarius: search for visibility by differentiation. Keywords: eccentricity; exoticism; rebellion; impatience; independence; personalism; innovation; modernity; originality; anxiety; stress; restlessness.

Axis 6-12, Virgo- Pisces, Desire for Cooperation and Integration

Virgo: seeking cooperation through service. Keywords: skepticism; consistency; thoroughness; neatness; perfectionism; competence; work; effort; modesty; simplicity; helpfulness; selectivity; practicality; utilitarianism; organization; method; logic; solidarity.

Pisces: seeking cooperation through integration. Keywords: empathy; altruism; generosity; complacency; contemplation; credulity; reverie; imagination; intuition; fantasy; romanticism; sensitivity; idealism; vagueness; melancholy; passivity; receptivity.

Elements and Modalities

As explained in Chapter 1, the twelve zodiac signs are divided into two categories: elements and modalities. The four elements are: *fire*, *earth*, *air* and *water*, and the three modalities (or qualities) are: *cardinal*, *fixed* and *mutable*. These concepts focus on the elements as the building blocks of all material reality, but they're actually confusing and produce contradictions within the system. I especially wonder why the modalities, or modes, are still part of the astrological model. And here I will not take into account any kind of metaphysical or pysicalist concept for the elements. It is better to redefine and thereby take advantage of this category because it is still useful and structurally coherent for distinguishing dimensions of personality. The three cosmosigns of each element are 120 degrees from each other, and those for the fire element are shown as an example in Table 3.1 (see page 44).

We saw that from a psychological point of view each cosmosign is defined by a set of traits, which can be personality traits. Some signical traits, however, are not exclusive to any specific cosmosign and therefore manifest themselves in more than one. When a number of these same traits appear in three different zodiacal signs, these three signs now form what I call an *element*: a set intersection of some signical traits common to three cosmosigns. Table 3.1 lists traits for each of the three cosmosigns of the fire element. This attribution of traits, which are personality traits, is empirical and based on experience. It has no mathematical (statistical) foundation and therefore should be viewed with caution. But it offers a sufficiently accurate picture of the differences and similarities between cosmosigns.

Table 3.1 Traits of the Cosmosigns of the Fire Element (common traits of fire elements in bold)		
Aries	*Leo*	*Sagittarius*
agressiveness, **self-confidence**, haste, competitiveness, courage, physicality, domination, **self-centeredness**, excitability, **extraversion**, hyperactivity, recklessness, impulsiveness, inconstancy, initiative, leadership, **optimism**, rudeness, **superiority, vitality**	haughtiness, **self-confidence**, authority, creativity, determination, domination, theatricality, **self-centeredness**, display, expressiveness, **extraversion**, joking, generosity, dignity, imposition, loyalty, leadership, pride, **optimism**, status, **superiority, vitality**	**self-confidence**, adventure, humor, lightheartedness, diversity, **self-centeredness**, enthusiasm, exaggeration, **extraversion**, flexibility, hedonism, idealism, irreverence, playfulness, liberality, freedom, **optimism, superiority, vitality**, volubility

These three cosmosigns comprise the fire triad. In terms of trait theories, people with an emphasis in Aries (Mars), Leo (Sun) or Sagittarius (Jupiter) should have a high score in these traits. When we say that there is an emphasis on this or that cosmosign, it means the result of a systemic or structural analysis of the chart that will point to the personality traits that emerge in accordance with the nature of the cosmosign and relevant planetary configurations, including the points to be highlighted. For example, if the trait in question necessarily involves relationships, the cosmosign of the Ascendant and the configuration involved in this sector will be much more relevant than solar and lunar cosmosigns. As will be explained in Chapter 5, there have been many misconceptions about this, not only by skeptics but also by astrologers. We can graphically represent the astrological elements as is done in the set theory. Each cosmosign then is a set and its signical traits are the items that comprise the set. Therefore, the fire element set is simply the set intersection of the Aries, Leo and Sagittarius signical traits that are common to all. Figure 3.2 is a graphical representation of this concept.

According to tradition, modality is defined as the qualities or modes of operation that the zodiacal signs have in common. In the zodiac, the three modes seem to indicate the possible dynamics of change or adaptation for the twelve cosmosigns. In modern astrology the cardinal mode–Aries, Cancer, Libra and Capricorn–denotes initiative, action, ambition, enthusiasm, independence, quick thinking. These traits are strongly associated with Aries and thus are characteristic of that cosmosign, but do not relate to Cancer or Libra. The same is true of the fixed and mutable modes, where the trait descriptions do not correspond well to all of the cosmosigns that compose it. The reader can verify this fact by comparing the description of the modalities given in Chapter 1 with the descriptions of the zodiac signs, which also appear in that chapter.

The Planets

The attributions of the planets presented below are empirical, because this is a first approach in defining the psychological structures that are activated by the planet.

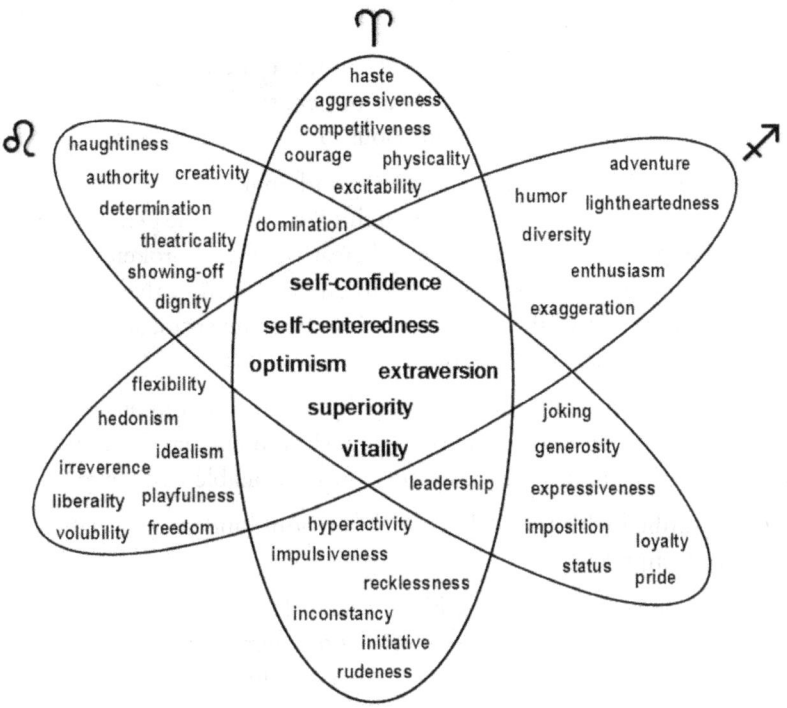

Figure 3.2 The Set Intersection of the Three Fire Signs

The astrological **Sun** is associated with the nucleus of temperament, with that which is most intimate and human regarding the individual's aspirations. The solar cosmosign indicates the needs that an individual must meet in order to feel accomplished or to promote his or her psychological well-being. Its "performance" or "activation" is in the conscious mind that thinks, plans and set goals. This is what the individual most identifies with, what he or she wants or needs to be, and is therefore his or her identity. This image, however, is not necessarily the one the individual projects or wants to project to the world. The Sun is not an indicator of social or interpersonal behavior; it points to something more essential, perhaps a more "authentic" and more individual dimension. This is probably close to the Freudian concept of ego.

The **Moon** has always been linked to emotions and feelings. In fact, experience sustains a Moon that describes the nature of the pattern of emotional responses. How do our emotions flow? Are they visceral or moderate? Stagnant or torrential? The configuration that comprises it–cosmosign, angular aspects, houses–can give us useful information. It should be noted that until the late teens the traits of the lunar cosmosign predominate over the Sun sign, with little variation from one person to another. This makes sense because it is a stage in which emotions are on the edge and behavior becomes hostage to its fluctuations. We must be very careful when doing an astrological analysis of a child or teenager as the solar cosmosign may not be easily identified in this personality that is still developing, especially if it has characteristics that are very different from the lunar cosmosign. *Lunisolar transition* is the term that can be used to indicate the transition between the lunar and solar cosmosign, when the youth begins to live his or her astrological Sun with more clarity. Then solar needs become more evident, or more conscious, or even more integrated.

Mercury shows a close association with the reasoning and linguistic expression or verbal communication. It's the way people use language and logical thinking. Does the person think quickly or have slow reasoning? Is the speech articulate, fluent and creative, or is it broken, nervous and standardized? Remember that this planet is never more than 28 degrees from the Sun, as seen from Earth. Therefore, there is a strong probability of it occupying the same cosmosign as the Sun, a situation whose psychological consistency makes sense.

Venus, in turn, relates to the need for acceptance by others, the dimension of feelings and the experience of love. From an observer on Earth, its maximum angular distance from the Sun is 48 degrees, which puts it in the same solar cosmosign with reasonable frequency.

As for **Mars**, it is identified with the body and its functions, and with sexuality. Other meanings assigned to it do not seem relevant.

The other planets–Jupiter, Saturn, Uranus, Neptune and Pluto–do not represent structures or aspects of personality or temperament, but somehow act on them. **Jupiter** has a stimulating, amplifying, dissipating, diastolic effect, and strengthens the internal locus of control. **Saturn** is an inhibitor and constrainer, and strengthens the external locus of control. **Uranus** acts as an accelerator for the system. It favors creativity, stimulates the intellect and also strengthens the internal locus of control. **Neptune** increases the sensitivity of the system, making the individual more receptive and less focused on self. This results in a higher level of empathy, and often confusion. **Pluto** stimulates the most primitive drives: fear of death, security, domination and sex in the sense of the perpetuation of the person through children, a probable unconscious mechanism for avoidance of death.

Houses

In the traditional astrology of Morin de Villefranche the houses had the task of personalizing the planetary effect, i.e., showing the manifestation of the influence of different planetary configurations. In other words, it showed the kinds of events that would be experienced, as well as their qualities, whether positive or negative. An astrologer, it was hoped, would reveal to the client if he or she would succeed or not in different aspects of life: business, money, health, family, love. It was a reading directed at possible events that could occur during the life of the client, and each fact belonged to a particular aspect of life represented by one of the twelve houses. Remembering what was stated in Chapter 1, if the theme was the professional sphere, for example, the tenth house or Midheaven would be analyzed, or the sixth house if it included anything regarding employment or relationships with employees, assistants or subordinates. If the problem were assets, property, money, the second house would be examined, and so on.

It is important to distinguish the role of the cosmosigns from the role of the houses. The zodiac signs provide valuable information about the various aspects of personality as they influence the five celestial bodies that act as direct astrological indicators of temperament: Sun, Moon, Mercury, Venus and Mars. With the houses it is the environmental factor that symbolically seems to materialize in the astrological chart. This, however, causes a great misunderstanding, which is to think that the astrological phenomenon involves the factual reality of the external world, and that it might tell us something about it. Without going into what would be a long and arduous discussion of the concept of "reality," remember that the astrological chart is, on some level, the representation of the personality traits of the individual, where you can infer much of his or her behavioral predispositions. In other words, this means how the individual reacts or responds to environmental stimuli. It is therefore the individual's own way of feeling, thinking, evaluating and acting in the world, or rather the tendencies that he or she shows regardless of socio-cultural influences. The end result (the whole personality) is a link between these two levels of behavioral determination: the biological/innate and cultural/acquired. The astrological factor seems to come after what was biologically inherited and before environmental conditioning, but we do not know the possible relationship between genetics and astrology.

Regarding the houses including the environmental factor, this refers to the ability to identify or recognize the environmental reality that exists within every living being, and living beings are but an evolutionary differentiation of the physical environment. Biological entities have phylogenetically programmed responses to certain environmental stimuli, which is the same as saying that they automatically interpret natural signs. The astrological houses are not real aspects of the physical environment–in this case cultural and social environment–although they refer to it. It is useless to sustain an identity relationship between this astrological categorization and the variations occurring in the outside world. In principle nothing can be said astrologically about objective reality itself, or better still, about things that happen before they become the object of perception and significance. Our constitution, both physical and psychological, presupposes adaptation to the environment.

If the houses do not represent the external physical world, whether natural or artificial (cultural), what are they? There are two concepts that are helpful in understanding the astrological house: psychological environment and *Umwelt*. The first is a concept from Gestalt psychology and the second was created by Estonian biologist Jakob von Uexküll.

The psychological environment is not the external physical environment; rather, it is the result of a perception organized internally and applied to things in or of the world, i.e., it is the subjective environment as it is perceived and understood by the individual according to his or her needs. We could also call it the mental environment. This environment is not objective in the sense that it can be the same for someone else. Instead, the psychological environment is subjective, specific to each individual.

Astrologer Noel Tyl was the first to approach the concept of field, from Gestalt, to the concept of astrological houses (Tyl, N., 1978), writing, "The horoscope shows the *field* of the personality."

Referring more specifically to the topological psychology of Kurt Lewin, Tyl shows that even the geometric representation proposed by Lewin resembles the way the astrological chart is drawn. Lewin represented the person (P) with a circle around which a psychological environment (A) was formed, defined as the area of an ellipse. To the set **P**erson + **E**nvironment he gave the name of Life Space (see Figure 3.3).

Both the P space and the E space are then differentiated and divided according to the psychological dynamics of the situation experienced. Similarly, the zodiac is divided into twelve segments that represent the temperament, while the twelve houses form a map of the fields of experience or related fields that may be experienced. The division of houses, unlike the division of the psychological environment is unchanged in each situation. The psychological environment of Lewin is divided into regions of variable numbers, with each region defining a psychological fact that can be an observed or inferred.

Figure 3.3 The Life Space

The houses are also like a cognitive map. These sectors work as social, institutional and cultural domains insofar as the cultural behavior has been naturally selected and is a constituent part of human beings. There is no better example of this than language, whose function is adaptation, not to the physical environment but to a complex social environment already biologically presupposed. The ability to produce culture, therefore, is already embedded in our biological makeup, as this competence depends on a sophisticated cognitive hardware, without which it would be impossible to process information the way we do. Just as the cosmosigns allow us to have access to what would be, metaphorically, a map of the temperament of the individual, the houses tell us something about the psychosocial orientation of each person.

The concept of Umwelt, coined by biologist Jacob von Uexküll at the beginning of the last century, is helpful in understanding the domain of the houses. Umwelt (German word for environment or surrounding area; plural: Unwelten) is the way each species represents the outside world in its consciousness. This representation is made using the system of signs used by a particular species to interact with the physical environment, to map it and learn about it. This is a subjective perception, built according to the actual structure of the organism and their specific needs but anchored in data originated from the physical world. These data become sensory data (themselves, signs) and are duly interpreted, generating (other) signs. This makes every living being, animal or human, a semiotic "machine," a self-organized interpretant system. The active perception of every living being is the construction of objects of experience whose relations constitute the subjective environment actually perceived–the Umwelt. Therefore, according to Uexküll, living things respond to signs and not to causal impulses. They are interpreters of signs of the environment, perceptual signs that trigger specific actions. These, in their turn, are operational signs generated by humans or animals. We are, therefore, faced with signical processes rather than simple mechanistic cause and effect relationships. We are all active agents of nature, which means different things to different living systems.

If we can speak of an Umwelt for each species, we can also refer to individual Umwelten, especially when it comes to human beings, whose Umwelt is quite diverse and complex. Different individual Umwelten are, in fact, perspectives, perceptual arrangements, selectivities, values and different orientations, up to where, in fact, people can differ from each other. Both inherited predispositions and acquired predispositions involve behavioral differences. The *tendency* to effect certain responses and not others must assume, following biosemiotic reasoning, some differences in the configurations of the various individual Umwelten, which can be understood as naturally innate tendencies because they are genetic. What we have here are multiple interpretations in the recognition of incoming data from the environment, followed by distinct responses appropriate to the subjective value of each perceptual construct. Moreover, we are here very close to the concept of functional equivalence formulated by Gordon Allport, who applies it on an emotional level.

Individual differences are therefore explained on the basis of minor differences of interpretation and valuation: cognitive distinctions. Here the cognitive determines the behavioral, or rather, the predispositions, because situational stimuli come from the environment and together with innate personality traits condition actual behavior. Therefore, each astrological chart can also be seen as a personal cognitive map, the Umwelt of that individual, his or her own perspective of "worldview" in the psychological, not ideological or philosophical, sense. Behavioral tendencies may well be inferred from this reading as a result of the dynamics of personality traits and already predetermined psychosocial guidelines. It is these guidelines that pertain to the meanings of the astrological houses.

Identity-Alterity Axis

This semantic axis brings the basic idea of the relationship between self and other, that implies acceptance or rejection, attraction or repulsion, alliance or confrontation.

First House (Ascendant): The sign on its cusp, the planet or planets in conjunction with the cusp, planets in the house and planets forming aspects with the Ascendant degree, in this order of importance, describe the social personality of the individual, one's public image and one's behavioral mode of expression that is projected on the world, the way one acts and interacts. As the interface between the internal environment and external environment, the Ascendant gives the individual information about the strategy of social adjustment necessary both for interpersonal and institutional relationships. The first house shows the most visible face of the individual's identity. It is not simply a "mask," but the aspect of the personality that is oriented to the outside, to the other. The dimension Extraversion/Introversion, for example, seems to be largely resolved into the configuration involving the Ascendant. The Sun and the Moon, in their turn, play minor, though not negligible, roles in this important dimension of the personality.

Seventh House: This represents the awareness of the other, the focus on the alterity (otherness). This field describes the interpersonal relationships as alliances to achieve something in common or as shared interests with a view to the same end. The other, however, can also be an adversary, enemy or competitor. It is in this sector that unions are established, be they partnerships or loving relationships. Traditionally, the seventh house includes marital relations, or any emotional bond of commitment between two people that is something more than sexual pleasure.

Possession-Survival Axis

What is at stake in this axis is security and the maintenance of material or physical life. Everything that belongs to the individual, including other people and what can be lost, is psychologically inside the space of these two fields.

Second House: Here is built the awareness of the means of survival, the resources needed for the continuity of life. Its meaning expands in assets and money. How do people handle that need? What does this mean to them? What kind of difficulties do they face? Will their actions be realistic and pragmatic?

Eighth House: In this field, survival and life take on a physical and visceral significance. The focus is on organic or physical integrity and the dangers to which the individual is subjected. Losses or provision of material resources are also manifested in the eighth house. In general it includes any psychological state associated with the phenomenon of loss or the feeling of abandonment, which can include losing or being abandoned by someone else.

Cognition-Communication Axis

This is an axis of intense information exchange. What is important here is to understand or decode the surrounding cultural environment and act on it.

Third House: The exploration of the cognitive processes and investment in intellect are part of the focus of this house, which also includes language in more complex levels. The search for scientific information, predisposition for study and identification with educational institutions where knowledge is transmitted are associated with an emphasis on the third house.

Ninth House: This field can be summarized in terms of social communication and the need to transmit and judge ideas and values for the community. The goal is to establish extensive connections and syntheses to understand the world and people's behavior and act on wide-ranging social levels.

Family-Social Function Axis

Connections and commitments between human agents are built on this axis to ensure safety and security and to perform social work.

Fourth House: The awareness and need of belonging to a family unit, or even an ethnic group, or a territory where a collective identity is defined manifests in this house. It implies the search for safety, protection, warmth, affection, and support in those we see as our equals, and who therefore can be trusted.

Tenth House (Midheaven): This house focuses on the integration in society through work, its importance, its value. What is the significance of the contribution of each person? What is the possibility of social prestige through work? What does one seek in the exercise of one's profession? These questions can be answered in this house of socio-professional achievement.

Play Activities-Affiliations Axis

This axis represents people gathering to optimize the enjoyment of life but without sacrificing or losing their individuality.

Fifth House: This house is associated with a sense of gratification, pleasure, games and jokes, entertainment and aesthetic experiences. It also covers children in general.

Eleventh House: This house is associated with relationships either in terms of friendship or with a collective group organized around common interests and ideas, thus meeting the need of belonging.

Labor Relations-Institutional Relations Axis

This axis appears to reflect the relationship between the part and the whole and the resulting harmony or disharmony in social or organic levels.

Sixth House: This is the house of labor relations, service and relationships of subordination. It is also associated with physical health.

Twelfth House: This house is associated with institutional relations and the consequent restrictions on individuality and freedom, as well as impediments that may manifest as disease and the perception of the collective.

The Syntax of Astrological Language

Chapter 1 included a brief explanation of how a birth chart would be read today. While acknowledging that this book is about psychological astrology, I do not identify with the Jungian school or even a psychoanalytical interpretation of the birth chart. My focus is on the personality traits and their expression in the astrological chart. I try to identify clearly and objectively the relationship between different aspects of temperament and astrological indicators, i.e., cosmsigns, planets (and their aspects) and houses. The intention is to present and clarify the basic meanings. In order to do this we need an astrological language that can be read at its most fundamental level. Not having a well-defined syntax means that this goal will never be achieved because the same chart can generate the most diverse and disparate readings, resulting in conflicting, if not completely opposite, meanings. But ultimately, what is syntax?

Dubois and colleagues, in their *Dictionary of Linguistics*, defines syntax as "the part of grammar that describes the rules by which meaningful units are combined into sentences. . . ." Simply put, we can say that these units are words that, combined or ordered sequentially according to the norms or rules of the language in question, construct phrases and sentences endowed with meaning. We know that changing the order of words in a sentence can change its meaning or even form a sentence without any meaning in that language. For example, consider this sentence: *The police officer killed the boy.* This sentence is understandable and says that a member of the police force took the life of a boy. It's pretty clear who killed and who consequently died. Now let us change the position of the words to read: *The boy killed the police officer.* Has anything changed in meaning? Yes, of course. More than that, the roles are reversed, reversing the position of the two nouns. This time it's the boy who killed the police officer.

Changing the word positions once more, we get: *Killed boy police officer the the.* This phrase no longer makes sense in English. It's just a sequence of lexical units. The sentence does not follow the rules of grammar, which every language must have. Moreover, rules pervade all human cultural creation and also natural phenomena and entities. In the case of nature, what humans observe are certain regular patterns such as the orbits of the planets around the Sun, the rotation of the Earth, or even the structures of minerals. Rules are inferred from these patterns, allowing us to say that the universe, in its organic and non-organic aspects, consists of ordered structures, real functional systems that only work because they reproduce an order. Or at least that's the human way of expressing what we see.

Syntax is not equally important in the two major astrological traditions–the Anglo-Saxon and the French. The first dates to English astrologer William Lilly (seventeenth century), reappears with Alan Leo, Charles Carter, Ronald Davison, etc. in the nineteenth and twentieth centuries, and establishes itself as an astro-psychology in the figure of Dane Rudhyar, who was also a theosophist. The second begins with Jean Baptiste Morin, also in the seventeenth century, is revived in the late nineteenth century by Henri Selva, reinforced by his student Jean Hieroz, and culminates in the contemporary figure of André Barbault, who is also an expert in astro-psychology.

In the branches of the first tradition, concerns about the syntactical rules are minimal. The reading of the chart is made by free association, or nearly so. It resembles the way dreams in Freudian psychoanalysis are interpreted, i.e., there is great freedom in the manipulation of symbols. On the other hand, the French tradition has stricter reading rules developed by astrologer and mathematician Jean Baptiste Morin. If in the latter we are interested in the syntax, in the first we see the birth of psychological astrology. First we shall deal with the syntactic aspect.

A Question of Method

Jean Baptiste Morin, a seventeenth century French physician, mathematician and astrologer, was a follower of the tradition established by Ptolemy in Alexandria in the second century AD. Claudius Ptolemy, distinguished astronomer, astrologer and author of the *Tetrabiblos*, was a staunch follower of the philosophy of Aristotle and all his work was based on the rationalistic principles of the Stagirite. Morin followed in his footsteps and developed a scholastic and judicious astrology, which many consider rigid, but which presents something indispensable for any knowledge system: a method. In 1661, five years after his death, *Astrologia Gallica* was published; this is a monumental work divided into 26 books and written in Latin. The work is certainly innovative and Morin had a strong personality, not hesitating to criticize Ptolemy himself, pointing out his "mistakes" as well as those of many of his contemporaries. Nor does he spare the astrological tradition of the Chaldeans, Egyptians and Arabs. From his own experience, he reconstructs astrology not only in theoretical terms but mainly by establishing well-defined criteria for reading a chart.

The significance that Morin's astrology has for contemporary astrologers is precisely what is lacking in many modern techniques of interpretation: syntactic ordering. Reading by free association, especially embraced in Anglo-Saxon astrology, allows the chart to be read in infinite ways, without any ordering rule. It's like an artistic composition and not a representation of a natural phenomenon. This makes astrology extremely vulnerable to the criticism of skeptics, which in this sense are correct because a language without syntax, i.e., where its elements are not ordered, could mean anything. And that's the same thing as saying that they mean nothing. The astrological chart is a text, or at least should be, and as such should follow rules of encoding-decoding that can decipher it. Totally discreditable to astrology would be astrologer A reading the natal chart of client X and saying that she is outgoing, and astrologer B reaching the conclusion that, in contrast, X is introverted. Or A says that Y is organized and disciplined, while B gives Y an undisciplined and chaotic temperament. Are they speaking about the same person? Are they reading the same text upside down? How can the correlation between astrological chart and temperament be read so that there is indeed a correlation?

To assert that a given personality trait stands out in a particular person, the astrologer should infer this conclusion by combining planetary positions in signs and houses and take into account the angular aspects between celestial bodies. This means that he or she must first decide which planet or planets are significant for this type of evaluation, which houses will be considered, if considered at all, and which angular aspects should be used. What, for example, are the determining astrological factors relevant to evaluating Extraversion-Introversion? How should they be combined in order to provide the information we want? How should the astrologer read the chart? Rules make a difference, which is precisely the difference between consistency and inconsistency. The lack of a basic consensus on chart interpretation and a lack of clear identification of certain personality traits, when quite pronounced, puts under suspicion the personality analysis that astrology claims it can accomplish. This is why we must emphasize the elucidation of the grammatical structure of astrological language and its relevance to possible correlations between astrological factors and personality traits. Let us begin with the rules established by Morin.

The Astrological Grammar of Jean-Baptiste Morin

It is in Book Twenty-One of *Astrologia Gallica* that Morin develops his theory of astrological determinations. The theory itself, whose foundations rely heavily on naive Aristotelian physics mixed with religious ideology, do not concern us. What is important is observing how judiciously and methodically the author shows these determinations and how chart interpretation depends on a properly ordered logic.

According to Morin, the planets influence people and situations in the sublunary world (Earth). The astrology in which he believed could predict events and make value judgments, could say if in any given area of a person's life things would work or not, would be beneficial or cause harm. But this does not mean that he believed in a fatalistic determinism without taking into account "the nature of things affected in the sublunary world," i.e., how to be specific about each entity on Earth, and its condition. For him, "the stars do not indicate the possible resistance of man against their power through prudence and divinely clarified reason . . . " except in cases where the event does not depend on the individual, such as in most accidents and almost always at the time of death.

Each planet, according to Morin, has an "essential nature," a semantic field of its own. The "action" of the planet, i.e., its influence, always occurs through the signs. The position of the planet in the sign is called the cosmic state, being strengthened or weakened, depending on the affinity between the planet and the sign it occupies. As was discussed in Chapter 1, the planet can be domiciled (or exiled), exalted (or in fall) or in some other condition of dignity. The influence of the cosmic state of the planet covers all entities in the sublunary world equally, but the effect in each one of them depends on the terrestrial state of the planet, also known as local determination. This is given by the astrological houses and the aspects between the planets, both of which can interfere with the planetary influences. Therefore, the position of planets in signs and houses and their aspects are the three main astrological determinations used by Morin. Although his analysis covers much more than these three components, they are enough for us.

What is new in Morin's work is the establishment of an orderly sequence of determinations that correspond to a reading sequence for the astrological chart. A syntax for that language was developed, and the final meaning of the astrological sentence is constructed according to well-defined rules of meaning, and these rules, it is assumed, must represent and describe the correlational structure that links the celestial bodies and personality, and is expressed in the astrological chart. First, it is the planet itself and what it represents that is taken into account, and then its sign position and what it means. In addition, Morin took into account the location of the planet ruling the sign occupied by the planet in question. This ruler was called the dispositor. For example, if the planet Mars is in Virgo, then its dispositor is Mercury, the natural ruler of this sign. Morin believed the position of Mercury on the map would influence the "action" of Mars and its full meaning.

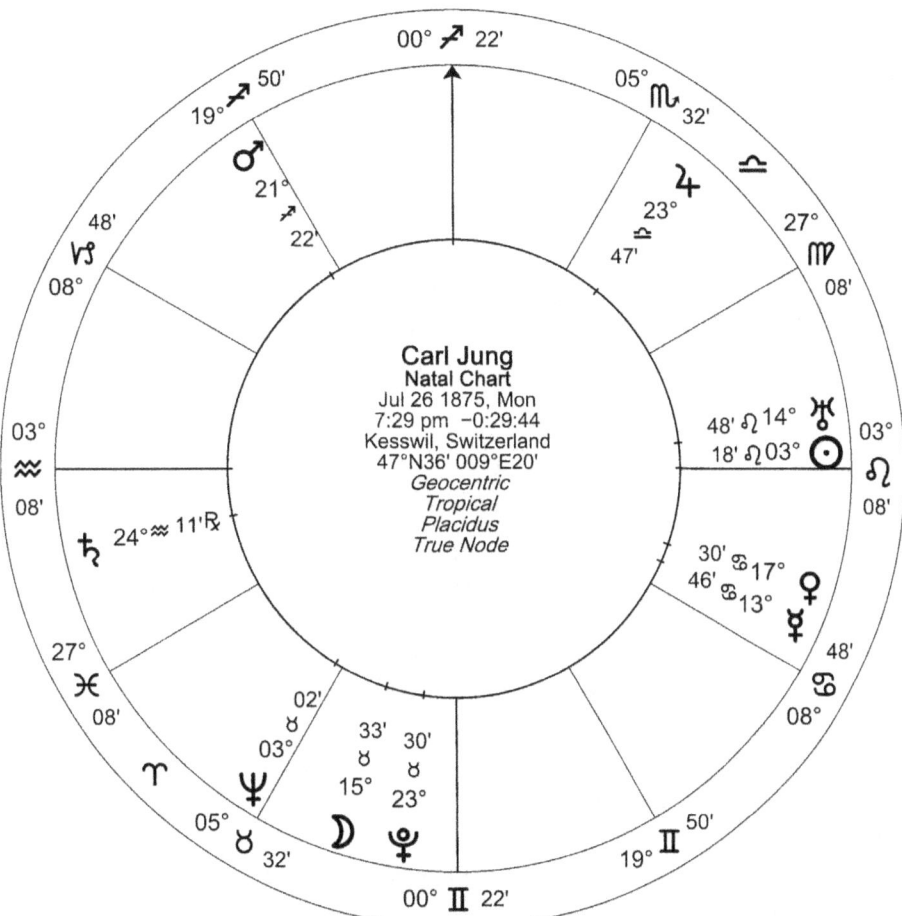

Figure 3.4 Carl Jung's Natal Chart, Rating: A

Then we get to the aspects. If no aspect is formed, the next step is to verify the astrological house that is being occupied, a factor that indicates the field or domain of experience affected by the planet, i.e., where the influence of the celestial body will be present in the life of a person who was born at a certain time at a certain place. The relationship of the planet with the cusp or initial degree of the house is also considered.

In a simple way (because there are other factors involved, according to Morin), this is the orientation to use in reading a chart. But how does it work in practice? Consider the application of some of Morin's rules in the interpretation of the Sun's position in the chart of C. G. Jung (Figure 3.5). Although unknown at the time of Morin, Uranus, Neptune and Pluto are included in the chart and their meanings are those given by modern astrology.

Astrology and Psychology

Jung's Sun

The first step is to define the Sun in the context of event-oriented traditional astrology without much concern for characterizations of personality. Here the star of our system is associated with honors, success, distinction, power, authority, dignity, noble feelings, etc., and also with the "life energy" that gives enthusiasm, courage and willpower. In analogy with the very physical sense of the astronomical Sun, the astrological Sun energizes the meanings to which it relates in the dynamics of the chart. For its influence to be positive and toward its own nature, i.e., to work effectively as a true Sun, without distortion, it must be positioned in its domicile sign, Leo. Aries, the sign of exaltation, and the other sign of the fire triplicity, Sagittarius, are signs where the Sun keeps much of its features and works well. In Jung's chart, the Sun is at the beginning of Leo, a very positive and advantageous position, which brings success, distinction and power. But in what sense? In which aspect of his life will Jung be successful? The answer to this question lies in determining the location of the Sun, i.e., the house occupied by the Sun. But first we need to better characterize the condition of the Sun, which does not depend exclusively on the zodiac sign but also on the significant angular distances between it and other planets, if any.

In Jung's chart, the Sun forms aspects with two planets: a wide conjunction with Uranus and a square to Neptune. Thus, the solar influence, and hence the semantic field of the Sun, is modified by its link with the semantic fields of these two celestial bodies; a conjunction is more powerful and prevails over a square. Uranus gives the Sun a sense of originality, creativity, innovation, utopia, and a break from what is conventional, and also disorganization and unpredictbility. Uranus has a strong individualistic nature, pointing to the creation of new ideas. Neptune rules dreams, daydreams, illusions, intuition, aesthetic inspiration, poetry, music, spirituality, mysticism, ideals and sacrifice, but also mystification and deception. Although a conjunction is a stronger aspect, here there is a balance because the conjunction is wide and the square is exact.

This web of meanings points to a particular field of experience in Jung's life, and makes sense especially with regard to things of the seventh house, the sector occupied by the Sun. Being opposite the first house, which is the sector of the Self, the seventh essentially represents alterity, i.e., the Other. More than that, its meaning unfolds, first in the sense of antagonism, confrontation and rivalry; and second in relationships, a union between two or more people seeking common good. The seventh house also includes commitment, a marriage or union that is long-lasting.

Jung's Sun is conjunct the Descendant and trine the Midheaven. This emphasizes the importance of this angular house and strengthens the position of the Sun trine, binding the meanings of the Sun and seventh house with the Midheaven: social position and prestige with professional activity.

How would Morin interpret this sequence of meanings? We have the following sequence: 1) intrinsic meanings of the Sun; 2) degree of concrete manifestation of these meanings, or their possible deterioration or malignant nature according to the zodiac sign; 3) interference from other fields of meaning (planetary aspects) for good or for evil; 4) primary field of experience (house) in which these meanings manifest; 5) secondary fields of experience (other houses) that suffer effects of this network of meanings by being connected to it through one or more planetary aspects.

This allows us to say that Jung was successful, with implications of power and prestige (Sun in its domicile), marked by surprises and sudden events or disruptions (Sun conjunct Uranus) and also bitter disappointments, mistakes, disillusionment, fantasies or deception (Sun square Neptune) in the context of relationships, legal challenges or personal issues in marriage or emotional commitment. The importance of these astrological indicators in Jung's life becomes even greater because the Sun occupies an angular house and is reinforced by the conjunction with the Descendant. The Sun-Midheaven trine extends a positive influence to the tenth house of success, honor, power, prestige and achievement.

For the purpose of verification, let's look at the facts relating to Jung's marriage and life. Jung married a wealthy woman who provided him with material comforts, and he had countless lovers and a tense, troubled marriage because of his marital infidelity. At the professional level, he was an internationally known psychoanalyst and Sigmund Freud's disciple; but he backed away from Freud and formed his own theories. His legacies were his impact on psychology and his broad ideas.

Jung's Minimalist Solar Configuration Analysis

The minimalist approach aims to describe an individual's temperament based on a thorough analysis of the natal chart, identifying its core (temperament) and inherent potentials. Based on this information, the astrologer can make several extrapolations: vocational guidance, counseling for emotional and family life, targeting the education of youngsters, interpersonal skills, analysis of business potential, etc. All of these possibilities include forecasts or projections in time that should not be confused with divination. The purpose is not to predict what will happen in the future but to project changes in psychological states and their likely consequences.

Now let's analyze the Sun in Jung's chart from a minimalist approach.

Jung's Leo Sun emphasizes traits such as high self-esteem, confidence, authority, pride, honor, grandeur, sophistication, ostentation, arrogance, creativity, humor, honesty and a strong attraction to the pleasures of life. Jung's temperament is basically characterized by these qualities. A fluid expression of these traits in interpersonal relationships depends on the Ascendant cosmosign. Aquarius there indicates a reasonable degree of consistency between what one wants and what is done in social practice, but if Capricorn were on the Ascendant, Jung's behavior would be far more reserved and defensive. However, Saturn is in the first house, which indicates a tendency toward retraction and moderation.

The Sun forms aspects with two planets: angular Neptune, which is square the Ascendant, and angular Uranus in the seventh house.

Leo and the Five Factors

It is in the Extraversion factor that we see most personality traits related to Leo. As explained in Chapter 2, this dimension (Extraversion-Introversion) measures the frequency and intensity of interpersonal relationships and the level of activity performed by an individual. Extroverts are typically communicative, sociable and optimistic. Leo represents five of the six facets of E:

- E_1 (warmth): tendency to be sociable, friendly, and amiable.
- E_2 (gregariousness): enjoys the company of others, having many friends.
- E_3 (assertiveness): strong personality, dominant and influential, leadership potential.
- E_5 (excitement-seeking): needs various stimuli, tendency to take risks.
- E_6 (positive emotions): tendency to a cheerful disposition, lively and optimistic.

Facet E_4 (activity), however, does not apply, which does not mean that Leo is associated with a slower pace but only that this characteristic is not emphasized in this cosmosign. It would be better to refer to it as vitality.

The Sun, however, is not a good descriptor of an individual's habitual social behavior, and the Extraversion factor relates only to interpersonal behavior. This personality dimension is better described by the configuration of the Ascendant, although the solar features exert pressure on social behavior.

The second factor that Leo is most represented by is Conscientiousness, which measures organizational ability and persistence in goal achievement. There are three facets of C that correspond to Leo traits:

- C_3 (dutifulness): tendency to fulfill obligations and to act with conscience, which makes a person reliable and responsible.
- C_4 (achievement striving): high levels of aspiration and ambition, entrepreneurial character.
- C_5 (self-discipline): persistence, willpower, self-control and determination.

For the Agreeableness factor, which measures the degree of solidarity or antagonism in social relations, Leo entails a high score in sub-factor A_2 (straightforwardness). Moreover, still in this dimension of personality, we would expect low scores in the A_4 (compliance) and A_5 (modesty) sub-factors, characterizing a person who is inflexible, demanding, stubborn, and arrogant and presumptuous in the more extreme cases.

Finally, for the Openness factor, which evaluates interest in new experiences, degree of tolerance and amplitude toward what is culturally unfamiliar, only the O_2 sub-factor (aesthetics) is part of the Leo field of meaning. High O_2 scores indicate people who appreciate the arts and show sensitivity to various artistic expressions, i.e., those who give great value to the aesthetic experience.

Leo does not correlate with high scores on Neuroticism, but the N_3 (constraint) and N_4 (depression) facets most likely will have a low score, which means rare moments of depression and anxiety, and plenty of self-confidence. This astrological contrast with the presence of Saturn in the Ascendant means a contradiction in Jung's own personality, with more frequent moments of embarrassment or depression than what would be normally expected of a Leo.

Combining the Sun and the Ascendant

The Leo-Aquarius combination indicates a strong desire for visibility and distinction. Thus, admiration, fame and social prestige were Jung's main life goals. The need to feel superior, hovering above the masses, was probably his motivation, corresponding to the sub-factor E_3, which encompasses personality traits regarding the need for domination, having an influential power over other people and somehow leading them (Sun in Leo). This desire for superiority tends to be satisfied at the intellectual domain of knowledge, cultivating creativity and originality, and with a considerable amount of unrest, independence and eccentricity (Aquarius Ascendant).

Jung was a proud man, pompous, perhaps arrogant, mentally active and tending to multi-tasking. He felt a great need to draw people's attention and to be admired, and was quite rigid and rarely recognized his mistakes. He had a strong personality, was determined and liked to present himself as someone sophisticated and with great taste. He enjoyed an active social life but always protected his individuality. He became angry when upset and was unconventional. He was bold and hated to submit to the authority of others. Although undisciplined, he was persistent in pursuing his goals. His motivation depended on a wide range of stimuli, and he loved novelties and was easily bored. He was not afraid to take chances and did not follow the opinions of others.

Jung had a strong sense of duty and responsibility, but only up to the point where his beliefs and freedom were not obstructed. The dilemma between doing what was socially desirable and a tendency toward disengagement and self-centeredness created strong tension. Jung was hardworking, entrepreneurial and ambitious, but poorly disciplined and often impatient and reckless. His own lack of discipline bothered him. He was honest and spoke his mind. His artistic sensibility was sharp, giving great value to art and science.

With the Aquarius Ascendant, Jung should score above average in the Openness dimension, enjoying a variety of ideas and cultural input and requiring a lot of intellectual stimulation; just above average as a judicious, competent and hardworking person in the Conscientiousness factor; and anxious in the Neuroticism dimension.

The presence of Saturn in the Ascendant is always a factor inhibiting social fluency, i.e., a factor of introversion. By itself it is not enough to make a person a typical introvert, but it fosters withdrawal, defensiveness and periods of depression. As Leo and Aquarius encompass personality traits associated with the pursuit of social visibility, Jung eagerly wanted to be the center of attention, but often felt trapped within himself. Thus, Saturn was a counterpoint to both the unconventional conduct of Aquarius (independent, liberal and daring) with regard to building a broad and multi-faceted social network where one can freely move about.

The Real Jung

Some biographies of Jung tend to get carried away by the myth, portraying him as an enlightened sage, a guru of the twentieth century. However, I believe the real Jung has been concealed and have thus focused on *Carl Gustav Jung: A Biography* by Frank McLynn, which seems the most unbiased and objective, as well as the enlightening *The Jung Cult* and *The Aryan Christ*, both by Richard Noll. Jung's book, *Memories, Dreams and Reflections*, in a kind of autobiographical compilation is also revealing and laden with a narcissistic intimacy insofar as Jung minimizes all that was not part of his inner "spiritual" life.

As a youth, Jung was quite arrogant and presumptuous. Narcissistic, he felt superior to others. As an adult, he was authoritarian and autocratic. He did not permit disagreement with his ideas, and lacked flexibility in dealing with people, although his leadership and charisma had attracted a large number of disciples and followers. An admirer of Franco and Mussolini, he was fascinated by Adolf Hitler, whom he considered a great shaman and prophet, and he greatly praised the dictator. Jung was also a sympathizer and somewhat of a collaborator with the Nazi regime. With his racist comments about Jews (Jung was an anti-Semite) he gained respect from the Nazis. After they lost the war, he quickly changed his mind.

Jung's intellectual output makes it clear that he was extremely creative and had an enviable intelligence. He read a lot and found it easy to create complicated concepts and fascinating theories, and to recycle ancient and medieval ideas. Although he was quick-tempered and often aggressive, he had a great sense of humor, often fun and playful. He was dedicated to studying and reading, but didn't neglect the material side of life. Avarice, his strong attachment to money, to the good things in life and the luxury, left no doubt about his preferences. Not by chance did he marry the extremely wealthy Emma Rauschenbach, which enabled him to fulfill his need for material opulence.

Jung's sex drive is legendary. A compulsive seducer, he took advantage of his position as therapist to collect lovers, many of them his own patients, who he seduced and then abandoned. A supporter of polygamy, he justified his behavior to his wife with outlandish theories, blaming his mother for his chronic infidelity and rampant sexuality. Thanks to his theorizing skills, he always blamed his parents for his faults. Despite the eccentric ideas and a rather liberal approach to sexual behavior and marriage, in other respects Jung was a very conservative, strict man whose political convictions could be described as extreme right-wing. He nourished deep nostalgia for a romantic and idealized past, a very common tendency among some intellectuals of the time. Jung hated the materialism of the twentieth century because, above all, he was a mystic, an occultist, probably merely disguised as a scientist.

Perhaps one of the factors that most discredit Carl Jung's theoretical construction was his profound mental disorder; he heard voices, saw ghosts and believed that he communicated with imaginary and mythical entities from the past. Like his mother, who was committed to an institution for mental patients, Jung probably suffered from schizophrenia, having used the psychic content of his condition to develop a body of doctrine extremely attractive to those who wanted to justify religious and mystical ideologies with supposedly scientific ideas. We cannot, however, discard all of his intellectual output based on these problems since his line of thought, though questionably confused and metaphysical, brings forth exciting and pertinent questions. It might be better to include him in the field of mystical philosophy rather than in the field of science.

The Minimalist Perspective

The term "minimalist" emphasizes the framing of the astrological phenomenon by limiting and defining concepts of a certain aspect of reality that can be objectively investigated in accordance with scientific rules. Astrology should aspire to a transparency that allows its inclusion in the roster of contemporary science. The road is long and the many obstacles are not easy to overcome. Regardless of its historic opponents, clinging to the past is the main barrier to the dialogue between astrology and modern culture.

The astrology I propose is minimalist mainly because it is critical of its original and traditional knowledge. Although we should respect it, it must not be blindly followed. It is true that the whole corpus has been naturally filtered through the experience of generations of astrologers. Yet there is a strong fear of opposing perceived unchangeable concepts based on centuries of use. Much in astrology involves outdated concepts and techniques that are used without worrying about validation; rarely is there a comparison to knowledge generated by science. Mistakes are not corrected. No errors are admitted. The sages of the past were never mistaken.

The need to streamline an astrology with techniques that do not work in practice and that end up being propped up by those that in fact support the confusing framework of this system of knowledge is what prompted me to devise a simpler system, and thus the choice of the word minimalist. My intention is not to superficialize astrology; quite the contrary, it is important to further investigate the core that fits well with the theories of traits and that also lends itself to a semiotic analysis.

Four

Biological Foundations

Biological determinants of personality are of interest for two reasons.

First, they could become an alternative for validating astrology, and perhaps even more reliable than the inventories and questionnaires used for psychological assessment. Although it's too difficult to establish biological measures that correlate well with the assessments of different scales of personality dimensions, it is a promising possibility.

The other reason is the search for a physiological intermediary in the astrological phenomenon that determines its behavioral manifestations, or better yet, the temperament and their preferred responses. Does the astrological phenomenon affect or somehow alter our neurophysiology and hence our response patterns? Are we able to verify this hypothesis? Or is it just the opposite that occurs? Based on their research, astrologers Michel and Francoise Gauquelin believed that children tend to be born with a planetary configuration that is somewhat similar to that of the parents, auto-inducing their own birth according to the position of some planets (or all of them). But what happens when it comes to caesarian deliveries? There are many questions and very few answers.

In order to address these practical and experimental issues, I will first try to address the relationship between biology and personality–and also astrology–in a broader perspective. We need a point of view and a model that can guide us both in the identification of structures or systems possibly activated by astrological indicators and in the interpretation of birth charts. One of the first astrologers to venture down this path was Carlos Fini, when he sought to translate into astrological terms neuroanatomist Paul MacLean's theory of the triune brain.

Paul MacLean and the Triune Brain

From his studies on brain evolution, MacLean concluded that the human brain is divided into three structures that reflect three distinct evolutionary stages: reptilian, paleomammalian and neomammalian, respectively related to the evolution of reptiles, early mammals, and recent mammals. They are three independent formations, but interconnected amongst themselves, which interact to form a functional whole. To this anatomical and evolutionist model, he gave the name of triune brain (see Figure 4.1). The older module, the *reptilian brain*, also called the *R-complex*, includes, besides the brain stem and cerebellum, sub-cortical structures such as the striatal complex and the basal ganglia, and is responsible for regulating behavioral routines such as the search for shelter, defense of territory, predation/feeding, basic socialization, hierarchy/dominance and mating. Evolutionarily later, the *paleomammalian brain* or *limbic system* processes emotional feelings. MacLean outlines six forms of emotional behavior: desire, anger, fear, dejection, joy and affection. The structures associated with emotions include the amygdala, septum, hippocampus, thalamus, hypothalamus, mammilary bodies and cingulate cortex. Finally, the *neomammalian brain*, the most recent formation, includes most of the neocortex and handles the so-called higher cognitive functions such as language and planning, and exercises some control over emotional responses. It is more developed in humans than in any other animal.

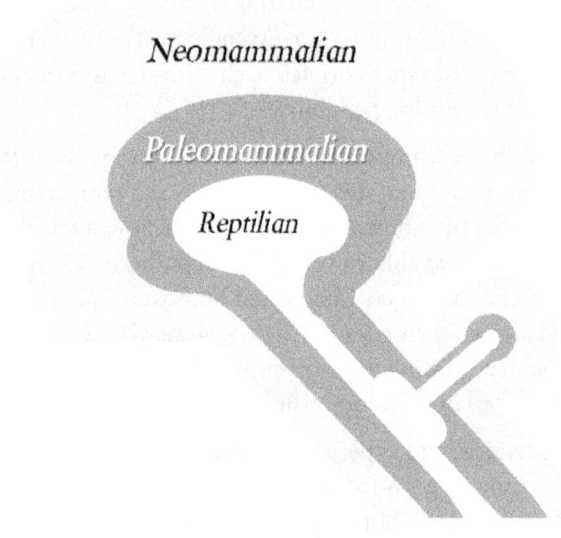

Figure 4.1 Schematic Triune Brain

The human brain is therefore a record of the evolution of adaptive functions ranging from control of body homeostasis through processing of basic behavior that seeks to protect and preserve the physical body, the orientation for socialization and relations of dominance and mating, expression of emotions related to caring for the offspring and warmth, audio-vocal communication, play activities and, finally, the more properly human cognition, such as language and logical-analytical operations. The emergence of mammals, which was linked to the development of the limbic system, marks the first signs of emotional attachment needed for the more prolonged contact between mother, and sometimes father, and offspring. Pregnancy and breastfeeding require greater intimacy and closeness between mother and child, and also a proper parental protection that makes possible the survival of a small offspring. When human primates emerge in the evolutionary scenario, they develop more sophisticated cognitive resources that allow them to optimize the adaptation to physical environment at levels never before achieved by any other species.

We have within us a whole evolutionary "program" that we share with other animals and that to some extent automates many of our actions, creating impulses that naturally serve as natural responses to certain meaningful stimuli. These stimuli can be threatening)negative(or pleasant)positive(. Social learning, among other things, teaches us to deal with those impulses in several ways, depending on the orientation of each culture, i.e., how the various human societies interpret the world and the role of humans in the world. Therefore, the expression of these impulses is largely modulated, regulated and guided by social pressures. However, whatever the characteristics of a particular culture, whether primitive or one of high technology, this arsenal of basic instinctual responses is ever present and can not be eliminated except in pathological accidents. And as we saw, each of the three brain structures identified selectively by MacLean handles a particular type of adaptive response developed through evolution.

These three levels can be referred to as *behavioral programs*. Thus, there is a *self-preservation program* aimed solely at the survival of the individual that is necessarily egoistic. The limbic system, in turn, operates an *affectional program* that aims to establish various forms of interpersonal attachment. This tends to be collaborative and sometimes even empathetic. Finally, the neocortex integrates information, or inputs, coming from these two more primitive structures, representing them symbolically and solving them with decisions or developing plans and strategies. We say, therefore, that the neocortex operates the *executive program*.

Triune Brain, Planets and Signs

Astrologer Carlos Fini empirically perceived that it was possible to establish correlations between these levels of neural processing and the planets. Dividing them into three groups, each made a match for one of the three structures proposed by MacLean, and therefore, as we will see, for a behavioral tendency or bias. Besides the interpretation of the birth chart itself, Fini also attributed meanings associated with the modules of the triune brain to the natal planets activated by secondary progression, primary direction, transit and lunation. Therefore, a contextualized planet in the natal chart could indicate the degree of activation of each of these levels and which ones would prevail if there were any predominance. He then extracts information about the individual's personality or temperament in a similar way to that obtained when applying the trait theories, and certainly with much more precision than traditional interpretation or even those of Jungian inspiration.

Fini put Mars, Saturn and Pluto in the first planetary group and associated these planets with the reptilian brain or R-complex, and therefore with a more primitive adaptive behavior, in an evolutionary viewpoint: search for protection, sense of territoriality, dominance relationships (hierarchization) and mating or sex. The first two, protection and territoriality, are assigned to Saturn; the dominance relationships, as they relate to control and power itself, to Pluto; and Mars is associated with sex drive and aggressive impulses in general, which is a component in the territory defense and often in dominance relationships. Therefore, when these planets are strong in the birth chart (appear in the first house or form aspects with the Sun and/or the Moon) it is to be expected that the instincts associated with the R-complex are intense or forcefully emphasized. If Saturn is a strong planet, the tendency is to manifest a defensive and cautious personality; when Pluto is emphasized, the person tends to be domineering and controlling; in the case of Mars, traits like aggressiveness and intense sexuality often characterize the individual. We could say that the emphasis on these planets makes the *self-preservation program* dominant.

In the second group are the Moon, Venus and Neptune. There is a link with the *limbic system*, the superstructure where different emotions are processed. The Moon appears to activate feelings of affiliation and emotional bonds, which is the search or the need for integration of the individual in the affective domain of a group, which can be the family, a band of friends, a religious community or larger social groups, culminating sometimes in the individual's ethnic or national identity. Venus is associated with collaborative relationships and so-called positive emotions, which are those that cause pleasure: recreational activities, desire (to desire someone or to be desired), love (as a source of pleasure), joy, social prestige and gastronomic pleasures. Regarding Neptune, feelings of identification, empathy, romantic love and sharing are part of its domain, and perhaps mythical-religious imagination or a sense of transcendence. As happens with the planets of the first group, the contacts of the Moon, Venus and Neptune with the traditionally called personal planets (Sun, Moon, Mercury, Venus and Mars) lead to a more emotional personality. Therefore, the *affection program* predominates.

In the third group are Mercury, Sun, Jupiter and Uranus, which correspond to the functions of what MacLean called neomammalian brain or neocortex. Mercury is the planet of language and in addition to stimulating curiosity about knowledge, it stimulates learning. It is also associated with discursive articulation and logical reasoning. The Sun is linked to the capacity of planning and objectification. The nature of the goals pursued by the individual and plans made for the future can be correlated to the astrological context of the Sun. The Sun is an important characterizer of what appears to be the conscious directing core of the personality. Jupiter, in turn, evokes socialization at the cultural level and also the search for prestige in the group, but in a different way from that of Venus. Its closeness to the astrological indicators of personality corresponds to a strong need for multiple stimuli and for broader social expression. Finally, Uranus is associated with creativity, with emphasis on individuality and personalism. This group "stimulates" the *executive program*.

As for correspondence with zodiac signs, which was not addressed by Fini, we can instead observe the resonances between planet and sign more or less according to the traditional rulerships. (I find the following traditional rulerships to be invalid: Mars-Scorpio, Jupiter-Pisces and Saturn-Aquarius.) The following are the relationships between cosmosigns, planets and brain structures (R = reptilian, L = limbic, N = neocortex):

- Aries-Mars: R
- Taurus-Venus: L
- Gemini-Mercury: N
- Cancer-Moon: L
- Leo-Sun: N
- Virgo-Mercury: N
- Libra-Venus: L (Libra might integrate the limbic and neocortex.)
- Scorpio-Pluto: R
- Sagittarius-Jupiter: N
- Capricorn-Saturn: R
- Aquarius-Uranus: N
- Pieces-Neptune: L

Counting, we have R = 3, L = 4 and N = 5. This shows a slight advantage for cognition over emotion and more primitive instincts, and may reflect the human's unique evolution among the species. This model of correspondences is useful when applied to the construction of a psychological profile that will emerge from an astrological reading. Fini has done elegant and intelligent analyses, and more importantly, done them with great precision using these correspondences. Finding possible correlations between measures of individual differences determined by variations involving these brain structures and astrological patterns would be a big step toward a dialogue between science and astrology.

In spite of some reservations to MacLean's evolutionary theory–such as the questioning of the development of what he calls the neocortex (Northcutt and Kaas, 1995) or the organization of the structures that make up the limbic system (LeDoux, 1996)–this functional division could shed some light on the relationship between astrology and biology or as a first approach to this effect. What matters to the astrologer is to establish correlations between temperament (or personality) and certain patterns observed in the natal chart of each individual. In Chapter 2 we saw some possibilities in that direction with the psychological trait theories.

Now it is time to focus on correlations between neurochemical, neurophysiological and neuroanatomical variations in the body and traits or dimensions of personality or temperament. In many of these trait theories, a biological factor is already presupposed and some of these try to identify and even develop neurobiological models of personality. What interests us in current research, more oriented towards anatomical, physiological and chemical measures in the brain and their relation to patterns of behavior, is precisely the relationship between brain function and individual differences.

Brain and Behavior

What concerns us here more than the brain-behavior relationship are the behavioral differences related to differences in structure, function and neurochemistry of the brain. Any feeling, perception or psychological state is somehow a result of processing that occurs in the brain, either in a particular region or neural circuits that cut across several regions and brain structures.

When it comes to personality traits, or temperament, many assume that most of these predispositions are of biological origin. This means that certain neurophysiological or neurochemical differences may act as determinants of behavioral *tendencies*. The question, therefore, is to identify those structures or substances, or neural networks that correlate with certain patterns of behavior and/or emotions. If the characteristics of the temperament depend to some extent on these and other biological elements, which in turn we know are genetically determined, personality differences observed in the astrological chart could be related to differences in these physiochemical systems.

As we saw in Chapter 2, each of the five major personality factors is formed by a set of correlated traits. Then we established the empirical correlation between the sub-factors or facets of these dimensions of personality and cosmosigns. Without this kind of conceptual approach we cannot do a consistent study of astrology and temperament.

Hemispheric Lateralization

The brain is divided into right and left hemispheres. According to the concept of hemispheric lateralization or laterality (left- and right-handed), some brain functions are represented in both hemispheres, while others occur in only one. Although popular thought says that the right hemisphere is emotional and the left is rational or analytic, this is not correct because both process emotions. There is an asymmetry in the activation of the frontal cortex with regard to emotional style that is a tendency to respond to stimuli with positive or negative emotions. Individuals with more positive affectivity show greater activation in the left hemisphere in the face of positive stimuli than do those with more negative affectivity, and people with a more negative affective style show greater activation in the right hemisphere when exposed to negative stimuli than those with a more positive affective style. To some extent positive affectivity is associated with the Extraversion factor and negative affectivity with the Neuroticism factor, or emotional instability.

The left frontal cortex is more active in more sociable and cheerful people and uninhibited children. In withdrawn and depressed people and shy children, the right frontal cortex is more active.

Amygdala

The amygdala is one of the most important structures of the limbic system. Located in the temporal lobes and made up of various nuclei, it is also called amygdaloid complex. Apparently its main function is to give (or recognize) emotional significance to sensory stimuli, especially with regard to threatening stimuli, recognizing them as such and activating the appropriate physiological responses that make up the fear and anxiety reaction. The activation of the amygdala, either in the resting state or in situations of exposure to unpleasant stimuli, has been correlated with negative affectivity: the more inhibited and more sensitive to punishment a person is, as assessed by questionnaires, the stronger the activation of the amygdala. It was found that the amygdalas of adults who were shy as children tend to exhibit a more intense response to unfamiliar faces than to familiar ones, as compared to adults who were uninhibited as a child. This means that in individuals who are more withdrawn and more likely to experience negative emotional states like fear, anxiety, sadness and guilt, the amygdala is more easily activated.

While the amygdala is best known for processing threatening stimuli, some studies indicate that it also responds to hedonic stimuli; that is, those that give pleasure being activated in anticipation of rewards such as pleasant flavors and money. Moreover, activation of the amygdala in the presence of pleasant images was associated with Extraversion, varying in function of this dimension of personality or at least according to some sub-factors of the factor E.

Hippocampus

Besides its role in mapping space, learning and memory, the hippocampus, in its ventral region, is associated with anxiety. Greater activity in this structure has been related to negative emotions during perception of negative stimuli.

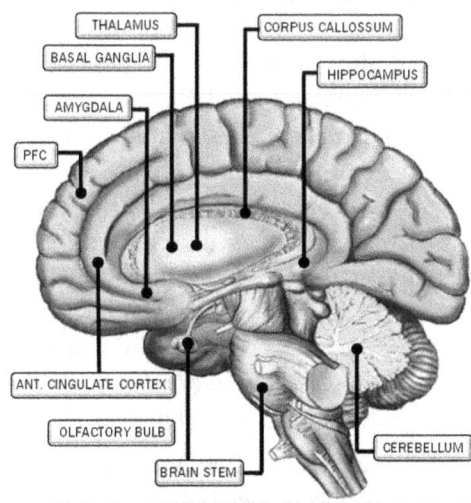

Figure 4.2 Lateral View of the Brain

Prefrontal Cortex

The prefrontal cortex (PFC), which represents approximately one third of the entire human cortex (Figure 4.2), is located in the frontal lobe and has the function of processing social cognition, which is the interpretation of social signs and the resulting decision making. Its *dorsolateral* region looks after the control of behavior, the representation of goals and how to achieve them and responses to environmental stimuli, while the *ventromedial* PFC articulates and integrates information on emotions, memory and the environment. For such functions to be performed, these two regions of the PFC have connections with several other brain structures such as the amygdaloid complex (emotions), hippocampus (memory), basal ganglia and pre-motor cortex (motor control), cingulate cortex (performance monitoring), the so-called association areas and parietal cortex (high-level sensory processing).

As seen in the section on the hemispheric lateralization, there are correlations between the activation of the hemispheres and the prevalence in individuals of negative or positive affectivity. The *right* dorsolateral prefrontal cortex (DLPFC) has been associated with negative emotions, while the *left* DLPFC with positive emotions. Thus, dysfunction or lesions in the left DLPFC, or a more intense activation of the right DLPFC in relative terms, are related to a deficit in the ability to experience positive emotions, which may mean a tendency to a more inhibited, restrained temperament, and with greater sensitivity to punishment, as well as a tendency towards depression. The activation of the right DLPFC was also inversely correlated to impulsive behavior. On the other hand, a more activated left DLPFC or problems with the right DLPFC are indicative of a temperament which is dominated by positive emotions: sociability, extraversion and greater sensitivity to reward.

A positive correlation between Extraversion and a more intense activation in the right orbitofrontal cortex, ventrolateral prefrontal cortex and bilateral temporal cortices was also found. On the other hand, activation of the orbitofrontal cortex showed a negative or inverse correlation with the Neuroticism factor, i.e., a positive correlation with emotional stability.

Other Structures

The *anterior cingulate cortex* (ACC) plays an important role in regulating emotional and cognitive behavior. Its ventral region, which has afferent connections with the *amygdale*, has been linked to negative emotions. Individuals with high scores of negative affectivity showed greater activity in the ventral ACC. The dorsal region of the ACC is associated with cognitive control and therefore the ability of containment. ACC lesions in animals have been accompanied by increased frequency of reckless behavior. The activation of the *caudate nucleus*, and also the *putamen*, by positive stimuli correlates with the degree of Extraversion. *Nucleus accumbens* and *caudate nucleus* also present, when activated, a negative correlation with the Neuroticism factor, i.e., correlate positively with emotional stability. It was also observed a positive correlation between the activation of the nucleus accumbens and scores on Extraversion. Caudate nucleus, putamen and the nucleus accumbens are structures belonging to the so-called *basal ganglia* or *basal nuclei*, which are part of the *striatum* (Figure 4.3).

In a study (Youn, T. et al., 2002) that related personality traits and glucose metabolism in specific brain

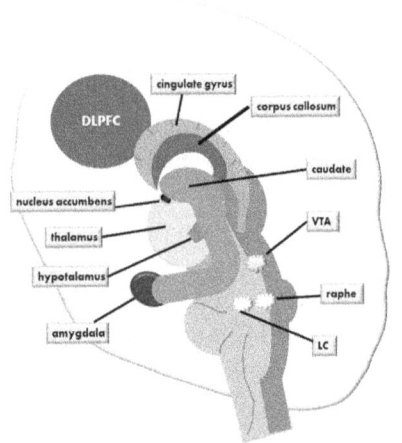

Figure 4.3 Internal Structures of the Brain

regions, measured by proton emission tomography (PET), the results correlate activities in various brain structures with C. Robert Cloninger's personality dimensions (see below). The Novelty Seeking dimension was positively correlated with the *right middle frontal gyrus* and negatively associated with several areas, such as the *substantia nigra, parahippocampal gyrus, right middle temporal lobe*, etc. The Harm Avoidance dimension was negatively correlated with *anterior cingulate gyrus* and with areas of right and left temporal gyrus. As for Reward Dependence dimension, there was positive correlation with middle and inferior *temporal lobes* of both hemispheres, the left *orbitofrontal gyrus* and left inferior *temporal gyrus*. Two years earlier, the researcher Motoaki Sugiura and colleagues (2000) had found correlations involving different anatomical structures of the brain and the dimensions of Cloninger. The patterns identified were very different from what was seen in the later study, perhaps due to the difference of method, since the first measured regional cerebral blood flow (rCBF) at rest.

Another study (Keightley, M. L. et al., 2003) examined the influence of predefined personality traits (FF model) in the brain activity patterns during induction to a state of sadness in healthy volunteers. Participants were divided into two groups: one for negative affectivity–high score in N_3 (Depression) and low in E_6 (Positive Emotion)–and the other for positive affectivity–N_3 low and high E_6. Only in the first group a more intense activity was observed in the *subgenual cingulate gyrus* (area Cg25) accompanied by reduced medial frontal activity. It is known that medial frontal regions are associated with the control of emotion, which makes sense for the group with high N_3 and low E_6.

Neurochemistry

When we say this or that brain structure is somehow activated, it means that circuits and neural networks involved in specific behaviors convey information that reach those sites, and also then spread to other sites. Any activation, excitatory or inhibitory, is the work of chemicals called *neurotransmitters*, which act at the synapses or junctions between neurons. When released in the synaptic gap (space between one neuron and another) by pre-synaptic neurons, they bind to receptors located in the membranes of post-synaptic neurons and generate impulses in these cells which will provide continuity to the transmission of nerve impulses.

Some correlations between certain neurotransmitters and certain personality traits have already been found. Although the various studies did not always show positive results, the relationship between temperament and neurochemistry appears to be promising as long as it takes into account the functional complexity of these chemical mediators, whose effects vary with the anatomy and physiology of the brain (Paris, J. 2005). Models that seek linear and biunivocal correspondences, and are therefore reductionist, inevitably tend to fail.

One of the studies used by most researchers in this area is the psychobiological model of psychiatrist C. Robert Cloninger, published in 1987 and updated in 1993. Cloninger has proposed four dimensions of temperament–Novelty Seeking (NS), Harm Avoidance (HA), Reward Dependence

(RD) and Persistence (P)–related to genetic factors, and three dimensions of character–Self-Directedness (SD), Cooperativeness (C) and Self-Transcendence (ST)–based on social and cognitive development, but that does not concern us here. The first three dimensions of temperament–Novelty Seeking, Risk Avoidance and Reward Dependence–were associated with three neurotransmitter systems: dopaminergic (dopamine), serotonergic (serotonin) and noradrenergic (norepinephrine), respectively. Other neurotransmitters may also be related to temperament.

Dopamine

Like norepinephrine, dopamine is a catecholamine biosynthesized from the amino acid tyrosine. Most of this neurotransmitter is produced in neurons located in the nuclei of the brainstem, such as the substantia nigra and ventral tegmental area (VTA), connected by pathways called nigrostriatal. These nuclei project themselves via mesocortical pathways to regions of the frontal and temporal cortex, associated with concentration and working memory; and mesolimbic pathways to the amygdala, septum, hippocampus, nucleus accumbens, etc., stimulating motivation, feelings of pleasure and well-being as well as the pursuit of reward. Recently a thalamic pathway was also discovered connecting the thalamus to the neocortex, striatum and amygdala.

According to the Cloninger model, dopamine levels correlate with the *Novelty Seeking* (NS) dimension. In this personality dimension, high scores are obtained by people who are very susceptible to new environmental stimuli, curious, impulsive and easily bored in routine situations. Translated in terms of the Five Factors model (De Fruyt et al., 2000), there are positive correlations with the facets E_1 (Warmth), E_2 (Gregariousness), E_5 (Excitement Seeking), E_6 (Positive Emotions), O_3 (Feelings) and O_4 (Actions), and negative correlation, or inverse, with C_2 (Order), C_3 (Dutifulness), C6 (Deliberation) and A_5 (Modesty). Low levels of dopamine were also associated with depression, which may mean a negative correlation with N_3 (Depression), which, however, does not appear in the study of De Fruyt and associates.

Serotonin

Having as its precursor the amino acid tryptophan, serotonin is produced in the so-called rafe nuclei, located in the midline of the brainstem. The serotonergic pathways project into many brain structures: the prefrontal cortex, hippocampus, basal ganglia, limbic system, hypothalamus, etc. Its functions are many, but what interests us most is its role as mediator of the behavior inhibition system. Several studies indicate that levels of this neurotransmitter are related to the *Harm Avoidance* (HA) dimension, which measures the tendency to move away from threatening situations or stimuli and to inhibition at the prospect of punishment. Individuals with high scores in HA tend to be fearful, inhibited, shy and cautious. At the other extreme are the daredevils and those prone to aggressive behavior. According to some studies, concentrations of serotonin metabolites are inversely related to aggressive behavior. Low levels of serotonin are also associated with depression. Many antidepressants work by increasing the availability of serotonin in the synapses.

As in the case of NS, traces of HA may correspond to some aspects of the Five Factors model. Positive correlations probably occur with much of the Neuroticism dimension. With Extraversion and Agreeableness factors, the correlations are positive.

Norepinephrine

Also known as noradrenaline, norepinephrine has dopamine as a precursor and is produced in the pons (locus coeruleus) and bulb, structures of the brainstem. The noradrenergic pathways project into the neocortex (prefrontal cortex), hypothalamus, amygdala, hippocampus and the spinal cord.

Cloninger associated this neurotransmitter with the *Reward Dependence* (RD) dimension, which measures the tendency to respond intensely to signals of reward. Individuals with high scores in RD tend to be sentimental, sensitive, affectionate, open to communication with other people and dependent on the approval of others. From the standpoint of the Five Factors model, these traits are found in E_1 (Warmth), E_2 (Gregariousness), A_3 (Altruism), A_4 (Compliance), A_6 (Tender-mindedness), O_1 (Fantasy) and O_3 (Feelings). The negative correlations, in turn, are with the factors Conscientiousness and Neuroticism, but not with N_5 (Impulsiveness).

In the Cloninger model, *Persistence* (P) was a subscale of RD (Reward Dependence) which became an independent dimension. The traits that compose it are similar to the Conscientiousness factor and also sub-factor E_4 (Activity).

Oxytocin

Oxytocin is a neuropeptide produced in the hypothalamus and released in several brain areas, including hippocampus, amygdala, lateral septum, caudate nucleus and anterior olfactory nucleus. Besides being a chemical mediator in the central nervous system, it is a hormone that affects uterine contractions during childbirth and in the stimulation of mammary glands for breastfeeding.

Several studies have linked oxytocin, and sometimes vasopressin, to affiliative behavior, to maternal (and paternal) care, the feelings of love and generosity, as well as the degree of trust and reciprocity among strangers. In animals, injections of oxytocin reduced levels of cortisol in the blood and therefore stress. Anxiolytic effects were also recorded. Deficits of oxytocin may lead to autistic behavior. This substance, therefore, seems related to the RD (*Reward Dependence*) dimension.

Glutamate

Belonging to the class of nonessential amino acids, i.e., those that are synthesized by the organisms themselves, glutamate also serves as excitatory neurotransmitter in the central nervous system. Negative correlations between concentrations of glutamate in the anterior cingulate cortex (ACC) and scores on the *Sensation Seeking* scale (a construct similar to NS) were found with the use of proton magnetic resonance. As seen above, this means that the ACC has inhibitory effect on behavior. Less significant correlations were observed in the hippocampus.

However, the correlations between neurotransmitters and personality dimensions were not always confirmed in studies.

Testosterone

Although testosterone is a hormone, not a neurotransmitter, the relationship between testosterone, aggression, and sexuality is well known. In fact, several studies have observed positive correlations, although not very high, between testosterone levels in saliva or blood plasma of males and characteristics as dominance, aggressive behavior, impulsivity, and extraversion and number of sexual partners. We could correlate it to E and NS.

Behavioral Genetics

The contribution of genes in determining personality has been widely reported in studies that compare identical (monozygotic) and fraternal (dizygotic) twins, and identical twins who were adopted and reared in separate homes. In both cases, it was found that the similarity was higher among identical twins than among identical twins than among fraternal twins, and there is a much greater correlation between the personality of identical fraternal twins reared in separate households than between them and their adoptive parents.

But how do genes contribute to the formation of temperament? What is the mechanism that links one thing to another?

Genes that somehow interfere with the action of neurotransmitters have been the main targets for research studies that correlate the type of personality to certain genetic polymorphisms. First, however, it is necessary to explain what the receptors are and their importance in the functions of the neurotransmitters. Synthesized within cells and stored in vesicles, neurotransmitters are released into the synaptic gaps separating the presynaptic neuron, where they are synthesized, and the postsynaptic neurons, where the receptors, which are proteins specific to each type of neurotransmitter, are located. The neurotransmitter, when binding to a receptor, opens ion channels in the membrane of the postsynaptic cell by changing the potential in that region, and thus can cause a depolarization or hyper-polarization, which means transmitting excitatory or inhibitory signals, respectively.

Once released into the synaptic gap, there are three mechanisms that can stop the action of neurotransmitters: the reuptake, which is the re-absorption of the neurotransmitter molecules by the terminal buds of the presynaptic neuron; the enzyme deactivation, which is the breakdown of the neurotransmitter by specific enzymes; and auto-reception, when a neurotransmitter in the synaptic gap binds to a receptor of the presynaptic neuron itself. These receptors, known as auto-receptors, signal the neuron to stop releasing the neurotransmitter in the synapse.

It is important to at least some understanding of how synaptic transmission works so we can understand the genetic variations in the coding of important elements of this mechanism. This is because the gene polymorphisms, or variants of a particular gene, will determine in part the different behavior phenotypes.

Although the current research results are often negative in associating a specific gene polymorphism with any one personality trait, in several studies many correlations have been observed and appear consistent with what we know about the function of neurotransmitters. Three genes (DRD_2, DRD_3 and DRD_4) that encode the dopamine receptors (D_2, D_3 and D_4) attracted the attention of researchers. The most promising is DRD_4, which is associated with the *Novelty Seeking* and *Persistence* dimensions. In the latter case, it was a negative correlation.

Still in the dopaminergic system, gene polymorphisms for the enzyme COMT (catechol-O-methyltransferase), which metabolizes dopamine, i.e., breaks down this neurotransmitter, reducing its availability at synapses, was associated with traits such as aggressiveness and the Neuroticism factor. Also appearing in such studies, the DAT1 gene encodes the dopamine transporter and is associated with the attention deficit hyperactivity disorder (ADHD), which is a condition linked to high scores in Novelty Seeking.

In the serotonergic system, the most important polymorphism for traits is the 5-HTT gene (or SERT) that encodes the serotonin transporter. Considering its two variants, the long allele (l) and short allele (s), the latter produces a smaller amount of transporter molecules that remove serotonin from the synaptic gap, increasing the availability of this neurotransmitter. Interestingly, individuals with ss or even ls genotype are associated with higher scores in Harm Avoidance and Neuroticism, two very similar constructs, as we have seen, and lower scores on the Agreeableness factor, compared with individuals of genotype l/l.

If taken individually, each of these genes, and probably others, contributes very modestly to building the human temperament–perhaps somewhere between three and four percent of total variance, considering that the genetic factors possibly represent a value of around fifty percent of the total variance of a personality dimension like N or HA, E or NS (Canli, T., 2004). It is expected, therefore, that there are gene interactions that may enhance, or not, certain personality traits, which some studies have suggested (Benjamin et al, 1998).

Final Correlations

We can now assemble a table with the various correlations that we examined in the last three chapters (Table 4.1 on page 76). After presenting the main trait theories and developing the first principles of minimalist astrology, I tried to ground the astrological phenomenon in a more concrete approach, i.e., a biological basis. We saw in this chapter some of the efforts of many researchers to identify neuroanatomical, neurophysiological and neurochemical determinants of behavior. More importantly, there were correlations between certain types, factors or personality traits and variations in neurological level. Although there is no great consistency so far, there have also been advances in correlations with gene polymorphisms.

Taking as a starting point the Five Factors and their thirty sub-factors or facets, it is possible to follow a route of correspondences and correlations involving various personality measures, biological measures and astrological indicators. So I believe that now we have better conditions to establish a fruitful dialogue between astrology and psychology, whether because we improved the astrological

Table 4.1 Correlations.					
Five Factors	Temperament Dimensions	Biological Structure	Neurotransmitters Hormones	Genes	Cosmosigns
Extraversion	+ Novelty seeking - Harm avoidance	+ Left hemisphere + Left PFC + Ventrolateral PFC + Right OFC + Right and left TC + CN; NA; right MFG + Putamen - PHG	+ Dopamine + Norepinephrine (E_1, E_2) + Testosterone - Serotonin - Glutamate	+ DRD4 + DAT1	Aries Gemini Leo Sagittarius
Agreeableness	+ Reward dependence	+ MTL; ITL; left OFG + Left ITG	- Norepinephrine - Oxytocin	?	Cancer Libra Pisces
Conscientiousness	- Novelty seeking + Persistence	?	- Dopamine - Norepinephrine	?	Taurus Leo Virgo Sorpio Capricorn
Neuroticism	+ Harm avoidance	+ Right hemisphere + Amygdala + Hippocampus + Right PFC + Ventral ACC - OFC; NA; CN; ACG - Right and left ITG	+ Serotonin	+ 5-HTT	Aries Cancer Virgo Scorpio Capricorn Pisces
Openness	+ Novelty seeking + Reward Dependence	?	+ Dopamine + Norepinephrine	?	Gemini Cancer Sagittarius Aquarius Pisces

> **Key for Table 4.1**
>
> PFC: prefrontal cortex; OFC: orbitofrontal cortex; TC: temporal cortex; CN: caudate nucleus; NA: nucleus accumbens; MFG: medial frontal gyrus; PHG: parahippocampal gyrus; MTL: median temporal lobe; ITL: inferior temporal lobe; OFG: orbitofrontal gyrus; ITG: inferior temporal gyrus; ACC: anterior cingulate cortex; ACG: anterior cingulate gyrus; + = positive; - = negative.

model and made it more liable to be validated, or through increased availability of behavior measures, which include the biological dimension. One must consider, however, that if the genetic load accounts for about fifty percent of the total variance measured by a scale of personality dimension, the astrological correlation might be only slightly more than that.

Reviewing the already established correlations, we saw that the factor *Extraversion* (*E*) measures the intensity of social contacts, how active the individual is, his or her needs to seek new stimuli and the ability to extract pleasure from the act of living. What we call positive emotions makes up much of the trait content of the facets of this factor. High scores mean that the person is sociable, cheerful, uninhibited, active, and loves to go out and have fun. The *Novelty Seeking* dimension measures similar traits: impulsivity, excitability, volubility and therefore partly overlaps the *E* factor. *Harm Avoidance* also seems to cover low scores on the *E* scale (negative correlation). *E* presents positive correlation with activation in the left hemisphere, the left prefrontal cortex, right orbitofrontal cortex, ventrolateral prefrontal cortex, bilateral temporal cortices, caudate nucleus, putamen, nucleus accumbens, medial frontal gyrus and right amygdala when faced with pleasant stimuli; also with the levels of dopamine, norepinephrine (E_1 and E_2) and testosterone; negative correlation with activation in the hippocampus gyrus, levels of serotonin and glutamate. Genes: positive correlation with DRD4 and DAT1. Cosmosigns: Aries, Gemini, Leo and Sagittarius.

The *Agreeableness* factor (*A*) measures the social behavior that ranges from the tendency to cooperation and solidarity to the tendency to competition or antagonism. Here high scores suggest a person is generous, selfless, caring and cooperative. This factor is very similar to the *Reward Dependence* dimension. It has a positive correlation with the activation of structures such as middle and inferior temporal lobes, left orbitofrontal gyrus and left inferior temporal gyrus; also with the levels of norepinephrine and oxytocin. Genes: ? Cosmosigns: Cancer, Libra and Pisces.

Conscientiousness (*C*) measures the degree of organization and persistence in pursuing goals. Individuals with high scores on this factor tend to be organized, self-disciplined, responsible and persevering. In Cloninger's model, *Persistence* is the dimension that comes closest to this factor. It is negatively correlated with Novelty Seeking and the neurotransmitters dopamine and norepinephrine. Genes: ? Cosmosigns: Taurus, Leo, Virgo, Scorpio and Capricorn.

Neuroticism (*N*) measures the degree of emotional stability of a person. Individuals with high *N* scores have high emotional instability, are very anxious, insecure, nervous, tense and likely to suffer from psychological problems. This factor is a construct similar to the *Harm Avoidance* dimension. Positive correlation with the activation in the right hemisphere, amygdala, hippocampus, right prefrontal cortex, ventral anterior cingulate cortex; also with the levels of serotonin; a negative correlation with activation in the orbitofrontal cortex, nucleus accumbens, caudate nucleus, cingulate gyrus and right and left anterior temporal gyrus. Genes: correlation with 5-HTT. Cosmosigns: Aries, Cancer, Virgo, Scorpio, Capricorn and Pisces.

Openness (O) measures the degree of tolerance to new ideas, new experiences and the aesthetic sensibility of the individual. High scores indicate people who are creative, original, liberal and tolerant to unconventional ideas. The dimensions closer to this construct are *Novelty Seeking* and *Reward Dependence*. Some structures related to NS and RD may correlate with O. Positive correlation with the levels of dopamine and norepinephrine. Genes: ? Cosmosigns: Gemini, Cancer, Sagittarius, Aquarius and Pisces.

Magnetic Routes

After all the possible correlations that we saw earlier, there still remains a fundamental issue: the physical connection between the heavenly bodies and human physiology. There are no easy or magical answers.

We know that the Sun regularly emits a flow of energetic particles consisting mainly of electrons, protons and ionized gases. Also known as solar wind, these emissions come as shock waves that interact with the Earth's magnetic field, producing geomagnetic storms and the phenomenon of auroras. With its core of iron and nickel, the Earth generates a magnetic field of two poles, behaving like a huge magnet spinning in space. Among other things, this allows us to orient ourselves with the help of a compass in relation to the north-south magnetic axis of the planet. This magnetic field, known as the magnetosphere, rises far above Earth's surface.

We also know that these geomagnetic storms, which usually last between 24 and 48 hours, but sometimes extend to a few days, cause problems in radio signals. More intriguing, however, are its effects on biological systems, since many of these have the ability to be guided by the planet's magnetic field and to detect small variations of intensity in this field. The ability to detect magnetic fields has been found in bacteria, bees, snails, sea turtles, fishes and birds. In the case of humans, there are studies on correlations between geomagnetic activity and suicide rates (Gordon, C. and Berk, M. 2003), incidence of depression (Kay, R.W., 1994) and many different human activities (Micek, S. and Micek, G., 2005). How variations in the intensity of Earth's magnetic field could affect our central nervous system is still a question to be answered.

The first researcher to suggest a link between terrestrial magnetism and astrology was the French psychologist and statistician Michel Gauquelin, whose studies will be explored in the next chapter. After finding significant correlations between some planetary patterns of parents and children, he found that this effect was more pronounced in births occurring in periods of greater disturbance of Earth's magnetic field. Apparently there was a link between geomagnetism and the tendency of children to be born in moments that repeat certain planetary positions found in the natal chart of one or both parents. Gauquelin believed that some planets have influence on the time that individuals with certain personality types or temperaments were born, whose determination would be genetic or, on the other hand, the baby's own body (and perhaps the mother) would be able to identify the planet that corresponds to his or her psychological characteristics.

As variations or disturbances in the Earth's magnetic field depend on solar activity, Dr. Percy Seymour, an astronomer at the University of Plymouth, has developed a theory that tries to explain both the direct and indirect influence exerted by the planets of the solar system on the geomagnetic field. His theories are developed in two books he wrote on the subject: *Astrology, the Evidence of Science* and *The Scientific Proof of Astrology*. Actually, Seymour's ideas only scratch the surface of the astrological phenomenon itself, but even so it is a line of thought that can stimulate discussion. For Seymour, a resonance occurs between the fluctuations in this field and the activity of neural networks in the fetus. Certain genetic traits would be in tune with certain planets and not with others. The child would thus be able to unconsciously map planetary positions and distinguish the heavenly bodies with which it was in tune.

What do we know about the possible biological, physical and chemical mechanisms of interaction between magnetic fields and living things? That is, how does this occur; how does the conversion of magnetic energy into nerve impulses occur? The evidence so far points to more than one hypothesis, whether in the case of spatial orientation or picking up field fluctuations. First, there is the strong presence in many living creatures of biogenic (formed by the body itself) magnetite crystals. Magnetite (Fe_3O_4) is a magnetic iron ore that is easily found in a natural state. In 1962 the paleoecologist Heinz A. Lowenstam detected its presence in a body, that of the mollusc chiton. Later, magnetotactic bacteria that are oriented by magnetic field lines of Earth were discovered. Other animals that seem to be guided by the geomagnetic field are homing pigeons (which appear to have magnetite in their beaks), seaweeds, bees, salmons and sea turtles. Evidence of a link between magnetite crystals and the nervous system are still few but it is believed that the movement of these molecules within the cell during the coupling with the field allows for the opening of ion channels, increasing the flow of calcium and potassium ions through the cell membrane. Biogenic magnetite has been found in the hippocampus of the human brain (Schultheiss-Grassi et all., 1999).

Other models have been developed, such as the reaction of radical pairs, which addresses the biological effects of magnetic fields on enzymatic reactions in the cell; resonance models, which consider the energy absorption of a weak magnetic field by calcium or potassium ions, thus altering the permeability of cell membrane ion channels; electromagnetic induction; and through the mediation of the hormone melatonin, released by the pineal gland, an organ that seems sensitive to variations of the geomagnetic field. Melatonin plays an important role in the regulation of circadian cycles, and levels of this hormone after birth are associated with certain aspects of physiological and behavioral development. It was found that administration of melatonin to newborn animals may cause effects that manifest themselves in adulthood, with changes in sexual development, exploratory and maternal behavior (McGillion, F., 2002).

In fact there are interesting possibilities that open up with the likely effects of resonance involving

Sun, Moon, planets and the Earth's magnetic field. Their interaction with the nervous system at birth, however, is highly speculative. Much still needs to be explained so that astrology can make sense in this line of thought. Furthermore, the astrological phenomenon is perhaps something more modest than the mantic system developed by tradition. Still, this theory seems unsatisfactory. At best it could be just the tip of a huge iceberg.

The Effect of Macroscopic Fluctuations

In the mid 1950s, Russian biophysicist S. E. Shnoll, working with measurements of biochemical reactions, observed a strange result. The distribution of these measures, which should be random, at times was amazingly similar in the fine structure of their graphs (histograms). In other experiments, using different compounds, the same regularity appeared in the shape of the histograms. In 1979, Shnoll and colleagues obtained similar structures in independent measurements of radioactive decay of plutonium isotope 239 (239Pu). All these experiments were reproduced several times with different techniques and involving phenomena of different natures. Thus, processes of different natures resulted in similar patterns, with the probability of random occurrence being extremely small. This means that external agents could be causing effects that were only identified in the fine structure of the histograms.

The recurrence of similar graphic shapes diminished with time, but they were again observed in periods of 24 hours, 27 days and 365 days, regardless of the nature of the phenomenon and distance. Measurements made in laboratories separated by many miles also varied synchronously and in the referred periods, so the effect is independent of location. The periodicity, distance and variety of techniques make even less unlikely explanations based on chance or in possible artifacts. What can be inferred from these "coincidences"? First, the results are not in agreement with presupposed theories. Any student knows, for example, that the radioactive decay of particles, α, β and γ is a purely random phenomenon. But, it is not what the histograms in the experiments of Shnoll and his colleagues show. And why would biological, chemical and physical measurements performed at the same time or at certain times, present similar graphs?

The answers to these unexpected fluctuations appear to be in cosmophysical factors. The frequencies involved clearly point to the rotation period (24 hours) and orbit (365 days) of the Earth, and the synodic cycle of the Sun relative to the Earth (27.28 days). Shnoll also found differences between patterns for the solar day (1,440 minutes) and the sidereal day (1,436 minutes). In later works, the Russian scientist had more surprises. Measurements made at different geographical locations, with different processes–α activity of ^{239}Pu, γ activity of 137Cs, oscillations of the Earth's crust–showed during the New Moon a variety of fluctuations with the same characteristics: histograms with almost the same shape at the exact moment of conjunction. Eight New Moons were evaluated between 2000 and 2001. Solar eclipses and the time of sunrise and sunset also showed characteristic histograms. Other experiments, in which the radioactive emissions were made with collimators, showed that these results depend on the direction of emission in space.

The effects observed were called macroscopic fluctuations and suggest, besides the heterogeneity of time, the anisotropy of space, according to Shnoll, perhaps caused by gravitational waves involving the Sun-Earth-Moon system. Another interpretation (Vezzoli, GC, 2008) prefers the external action of elementary particles, with momentum transfer, based on a model of quantum gravity. Whatever it is, the astrological phenomenon has always implied a variation in the quality of time and a topology of properties still unknown. For astrology, not only the personality and human behavior, but social and even geological phenomena are influenced by the heavenly bodies from their positions in the sky. The zodiacal space is an anisotropic space, i.e., whose properties vary along its length. Astrological time is not homogeneous, so it can have several meanings in its duration.

The findings of Shnoll and his colleagues may bring even more surprises and challenges. I believe that new properties of space-time may come to light, making astrology more viable in the eyes of science.

We are still far from being able to explain in physical terms the nature of the relationship between the astronomical-astrological configuration at the moment of the birth of an individual and the dynamics of his or her personality traits. As for now I rule out the metaphysical explanations of Jung involving the almost magical concept of synchronicity, so it would be appropriate to replace them by a more convincing explanation of naturalistic nature, with the implications of cause and effect, or better yet, a semiotic model, which seems more promising. Unfortunately, we have not yet built a model that takes into account the correlations we observe. This great gap, however, should not prevent us from going forward, particularly with respect to factors that, in their variation, contribute to the existence of individual differences.

Astrology is basically a tool used to explore these differences and to characterize them. The matrices of the various temperaments that can be identified in astrological analysis are obviously not due to immediate environmental influences, nor do they point to certain social situations that shall be experienced by the person. It has already become clear that what is at stake here are personality traits and their pre-dispositional character, behavior patterns that recur throughout life and are responsible for much of the identity of the individual. Time passes and yet this person can be identified by a baseline of behavior.

As for physical explanations that might link the celestial bodies and the temperament and behavior of individuals on Earth, they logically depend on the development of physical and chemical sciences and the ability of scientist-astrologers to visualize relationships with astrological phenomenon. Astrologers cannot be mere observers, hoping that science finally acknowledges the existence of this mysterious connection between sky and earth. They should be participants.

Chapter 5

Michel Gauquelin's Research

The 1955 publication of *The Influence of the Stars* by French psychologist Michel Gauquelin was a milestone in astrology. The book presents the results of his research on the validity of astrological correlations. As a child, Gauquelin had a real fascination for astrology. At age seven, he knew the sun sign of his classmates if they told him their date of birth. At ten he learned to calculate the Ascendant with his father, Roland Gauquelin, a dentist. And so he reached adolescence devouring books on astrology. No wonder his school colleagues called him Nostradamus. But the prestige he obtained from the girls made up for any jokes or teasing by the boys.

As the young Michel matured, there grew within him the need for evidence and scientific demonstrations. He launched himself in search of dates and times of birth to verify once and for all if the claims of the ancient science of astrology were true or false. In his own words, "What little money I had I spent on stamps for letters I wrote to the many birth record offices of France, asking for times of birth." Gauquelin had in mind a survey of statistical nature and needed to gather sufficient data to reach a valid conclusion. Initial tests focused on zodiacal symbolism: the influence of the zodiac signs in the career choice and inheritance between parents and children. The findings were published after five years of work in 1955, in his first book, *L'Influence des Astres*. Up until then nobody had conducted research project on astrology that was as broad and as well prepared. And it is no exaggeration to say that today all of his work, including further studies, has not been surpassed in magnitude and quality.

Gauquelin begins the book by stating that he considers astrology to be "medieval beliefs, founded on arbitrary laws." He further adds that astrology is "a superstition, a survivor of an ancient animism." However, he argues of the possibility of an astrological link between stars and humans that he tries to prove in the second part of the book.

Gauquelin's study of heredity compares the planetary positions of the Sun in the charts of parents and their children, and in the charts of siblings. He also investigated the planetary distribution in the ecliptic for two families, including four generations. Gauquelin says that, compared to control groups, the results were still below average. Despite this conclusion, any astrologer with a good knowledge of the craft knows that in fact there is consistency in the charts of close relatives. The verification of consistency between charts of parents and children, and charts of siblings, for example, can be made if we translate the indicators of personality in each of the charts in terms of personality traits and incorporate them in an astrologically appropriate interpretation.

Gauquelin checked the positions of the Sun, Moon, planets, Ascendant and Midheaven for priests, soldiers, actors, sportsmen, politicians, painters, writers, doctors and criminals. Again, he was misled by classical astrology, which attributes to any profession or social activity an astrological pattern recognizable in a chart. The intention was to identify the individual's profession, but that was unsuccessful because personality traits are not equivalent to a specific profession. For Gauquelin, these results meant the "demolition of astrology."

Gauquelin's book explains the statistical method used in the other part of his research. Unlike studies focusing on the zodiac, he used the distribution of the planets, and realized interesting results. Studying the planetary placements of more than 1,000 physicians, he found that Mars and Saturn appeared more frequently in a rising position (on the horizon) and in upper culmination (local meridian) in their birth charts. This frequency in two of the sectors far surpassed what would be expected from a random distribution, and this proved to be statistically significant.

Other professions were also assessed, and significant correlations occured in the rising and culmination of Mars for athletes, of Jupiter for actors and politicians, Saturn for scientists and the Moon for writers and politicians. The same effect occurred in other studies, with the same planets appearing with much greater frequency near the eastern horizon and in upper culmination. There was also a small increase in the frequency of those close to setting and in lower culmination. The other planets, including the Sun, showed no correlation with any of the professions surveyed.

In *Planetary Heredity*, Gauquelin presented the results of a comparison of the planetary positions of parents and their children, using the same method as he used for professions. The planets that occupy the region surrounding the Ascendant and Midheaven at the time parents were born tended to reproduce in the charts of their children. Statistically, the values are significant and the effect on planetary heredity reinforces the result of previous research. This time Venus also appeared as significant in the correlations.

Gauquelin would find another interesting correlation between geomagnetic activity and the intensity of the effect on planetary heredity in terms of positive cases. According to the calculations made, the planetary effect was about two times greater when the child was born on days of greatest magnetic disturbance, i.e., the correlations between parents and children were more frequent on those days. If the delivery was by cesarean section rather than normal birth, the correlation decreased substantially.

In the late 1960s, Gauquelin took a new direction in his research. The results of two decades of work seemed to point toward a much more promising direction. Better than professional relationships with planets would be to connect these heavenly bodies with personality traits typical of people who are successful in a particular career. So he moved away from the idea of destiny.

Because Gauquelin's research found statistically significant values only in high-level professionals, those who reached the top of their career, the individual must possess certain characteristics that are virtually indispensable for a given job. For example, executives should take initiative and be dynamic (Mars), scientists need to be introspective and disciplined (Saturn), actors are usually extraverts (Jupiter), and so on.

Diurnal Movement

Due to Earth's rotation on its axis, an observer can see the Sun, Moon, planets and stars following a path on the celestial sphere. This approximate 24-hour movement is from east to west as Earth rotates in the opposite direction, i.e., from west to east. Figure 5.1 shows the diurnal motion of Mars for May 24, 1956, in Paris. That day, the red planet rose or appeared on the eastern horizon at 0h44, culminated at 5:33 am, and set on the western horizon at 10:22 am.

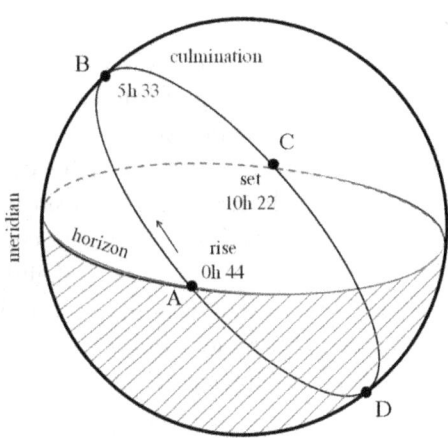

Figure 5.1 Diurnal movement of Mars.

In Figure 5.1 the two large perpendicular circles are the horizon and the local meridian. The movement of Mars is marked by the circle ABCDA. Point A marks the time this celestial body appears on the eastern horizon, crossing the horizon at 0:44 am. Continuing its journey, it rises in the sky to reach its culmination, i.e., its highest point on the celestial sphere, point B, at 5:33 am. Then it starts to descend to point C and intersects the western horizon at 10:22 am. From this position, Mars goes below the horizon until it reaches point D, where it crosses the me-

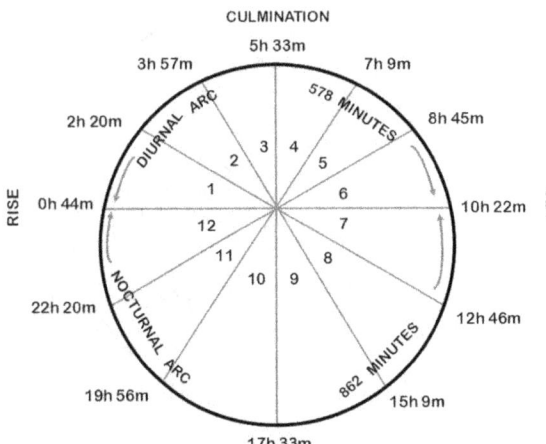

Figure 5.2 The Twelve Sectors of the Diurnal Sphere.

ridian at its lower culmination, located 180 degrees from the superior culmination. From that point it will return to point A, rising again.

What interested Gauquelin was precisely to determine the position of a planet, the Sun and the Moon at the time a person is born. To make a statistical calculation of the frequency of births at several possible positions, he had to divide the circle of diurnal movement into equal parts. Thus all births that occurred when a planet was in a certain region of the celestial sphere are added to give a total. Therefore, following the example of Mars, the diurnal motion of this planet is divided into 12 parts or sectors. Do not confuse this division with the division of astrological houses, although the positions of the Ascendant and Midheaven (upper culmination) are the same. In the future, Gauquelin also would use the Placidus system of astrological houses.

In Figure 5.2 we see that Mars was above the horizon for 9 hours and 38 minutes (578 minutes). Therefore, it remained below the horizon for 862 minutes, for a combined total of 1,440 minutes, i.e., 24 hours. Then divide the diurnal arc (above the horizon) of the planet into six equal sectors, each with 96 minutes of arc, and do the same to the nocturnal arc (below the horizon), each sector with 144 minutes of arc. The sectors are numbered from 1 to 12, with the first starting at rising at 0:44 a.m., the second at 2:20 a.m., then passing through the Midheaven at 5:33 a.m., at sunset at 10:22 am, and so on. If a person were born that day at 1:10 a.m., Mars was in Sector 1, slightly above the skyline. If the birth were at 5:15, Mars approached the Midheaven, but still in sector 3. The same procedure applies to the position of other celestial bodies. In samples of a few thousand births, the planets and luminaries are distributed among these sectors, occupying each of them with a certain frequency.

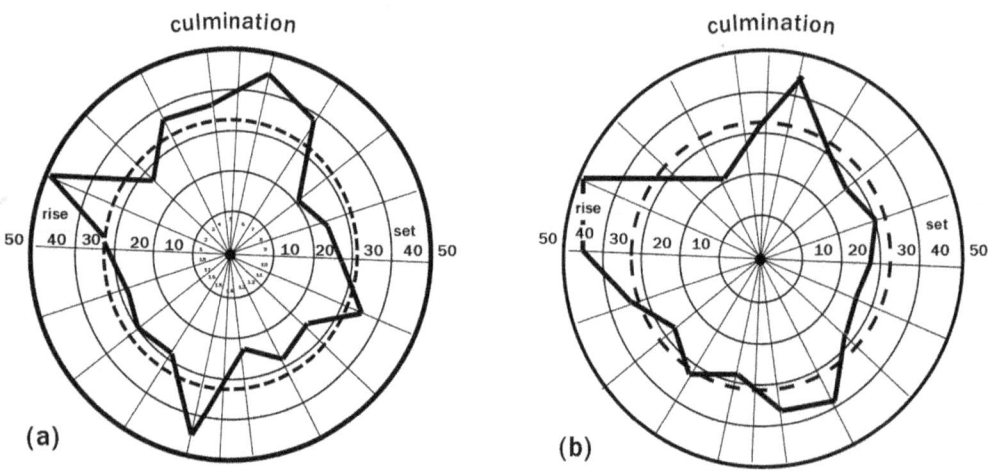

Figure 5.3 (a) Distribution for Mars Among 576 Eminent Physicians; (b) Distribution for Saturn, idem.

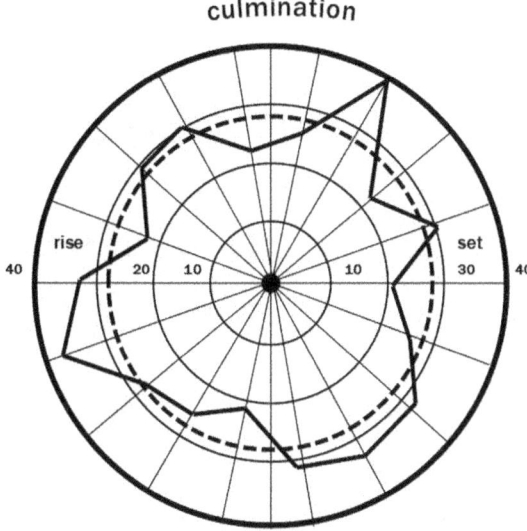

Figure 5.4 Distribution for Jupiter Among 576 Eminent Physicians.

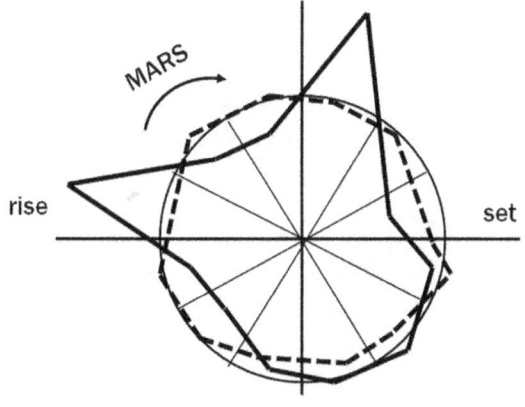

Figure 5.5 Distribution of Mars for Sports Champions.

Experimental Procedures

Theoretically, a planet would be in each chart one-twelfth (8.33 percent) of the time. If the distribution of births surveyed is within this average, with an almost equal number of births in each sector, the distribution is random. To statistically analyze the samples, Gauquelin used the chi-square distribution, a measure that compares observed frequencies with theoretically expected frequencies, demonstrating the extent of the discrepancy between the two sets of data. This distribution can reveal whether there is a statistically significant correlation between the position of the planet and a number of births. As mentioned earlier, the first successful experiment showed that the number of physicians born at the time Mars (Figure 5.3a) and Saturn (Figure 5.3b) rose on the eastern horizon, or shortly after they crossed the local meridian, was significantly higher than average. The frequency found for Mars was 21.35 percent and Saturn was 22.57 percent.

Gauquelin repeated the experiment with another sample, which confirmed a highly significant frequency of births when Mars and Saturn occupied the two sectors. Just as interesting was what he found in relation to Jupiter, whcih had an occupancy rate of well below average in sectors where Mars and Saturn stood out (see Figure 5.4).

Gauquelin then collected birth data of those who excelled in sports, politics, war, and other activities. Again, some planets confirmed their traditional meanings. The same sectors showed a higher frequency of Mars, and this became known as the *Mars Effect*. In one experiment, for an expected frequency of 253 births in the key sectors, or plus zones as he called them, the observed frequency was 327 births in a sample of 1,485 champions. Given the sample size, the difference in relation to the theoretical frequency, even though relatively small, becomes extremely significant. This is a deviation of more than 29 percent.

In Figure 5.5, we see a circular graphical representation of the distribution of Mars at the time of birth of 2,088 sports champions. The circle represents the theoretical distribution, the solid line, the positions of Mars, and the dashed line, the distribution of Mars in the birth of 717 common athletes. It can be seen that the solid line displays a peak shortly after the birth and the Midheaven. For average athletes, however, the pattern disappears. Systematically, Gauquelin found that this statistically significant result only occurred among eminent professionals.

Figure 5.6 shows the positions of Saturn for 3,647 scientists (solid line) and 5,100 artists (dashed line). The planet traditionally associated with introspection, discipline, introversion, concentration, appears shortly after rising and at the Midheaven much more often in the sample of top scientists. In contrast, among the artists, the frequency was below average

In Figure 5.7 we can see the distribution of Jupiter for a sample of 993 politicians. The dashed circle corresponds to the theoretical result of a control group. The same pattern is repeated. In astrology, this planet is associated with characteristics such as extraversion, optimism, sociability, expressiveness, etc.

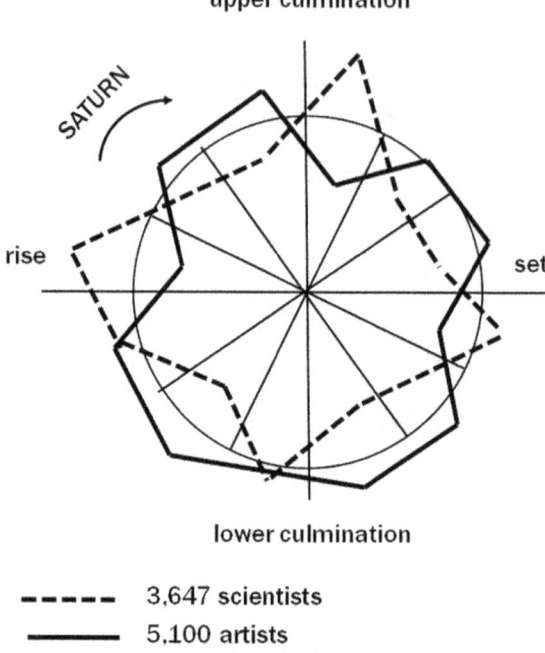

Figure 5.6 Distribution of Saturn for Scientists and Artists.

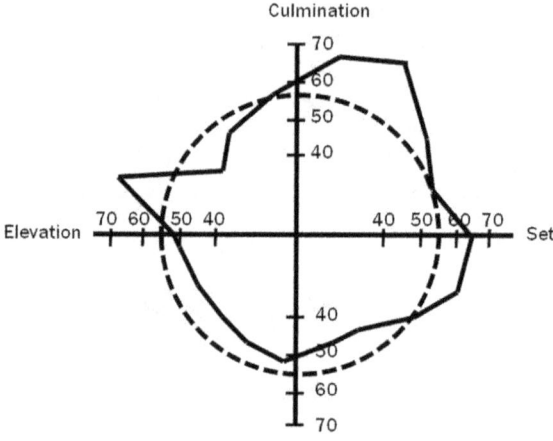

Figure 5.7 Distribution of Jupiter for Politicians.

Table 5.1 Correlations Between Planets and Professions.		
After the rising and upper culmination of:	*High birth frequencies*	*Low birth frequencies*
Jupiter	actors and playwrights politicians military leaders top executives journalists	scientists physicians
Saturn	scientists physicians	actors journalists writers painters
Mars	physicians military leaders sports champions top executives	painters musicians writers
Moon	writers politicians	

Personality Traits

In the early 1960s, there was a shift in Gauquelin's work. Instead of planets and professions, he realized that there was a more effective underlying relationship between planets and personality traits. This new relationship could explain why a recurring distribution pattern only appeared in samples of high-level professionals, and not in average people.

Successful people often have well accentuated personality traits that allow them to stand out, and the research results, which suggested something like a destiny set by the planets, were perhaps not so strange. Maybe they were showing a certain type of behavior associated with the performance of certain professions. In this case the planet would have nothing to do with this or that profession but with certain personality characteristics. Applying this logic, it makes sense that people who were more aggressive, determined, self-assertive, competitive and who had initiative were more likely to excel in careers that require such attitudes: the military, business and athletics. In this case, we can say that Mars is dominant in sectors one and four. If the Moon dominates, professions are writing and politics: imagination, sensitivity, emotionality, volubility and desire for popularity are, among others, the traits that define the nature of the Moon. Table 5.1 summarizes the qualitative correlations between planets and successful professionals.

To support his hypothesis (that the position of a planet at the time and place of birth is related to certain personality types) Gauquelin used the biographical information of eminent professionals whose birth data he had on hand. Starting from, therefore, the descriptions produced by others, he would extract the words that the author used to characterize the personality or behavior of the subject. Terms such as passionate, serious, stubborn and aggressive were examples of traits that served to typify a person.

To clarify, he was trying to find a correlation between planets and personality traits, not professions. In charts of strong-willed athletes, Mars appeared twice as frequently in key sectors than in the case of weak-willed ones. Very social actors were born with Jupiter much more frequently in key sectors than those who were less communicative. Introspective scientists were more often born when Saturn was in one of those sectors than were more extraverted scientists. And finally, the Moon showed up more frequently in the sectors one and four for exceptionally sensitive and imaginative writers.

There arose, therefore, four planetary factors that somehow acted as determinants for personality or simply as correlates, and even more important, these types reproduced the meanings of planetary astrological tradition. The observations of the ancients, though anecdotal and without the sophistication of modern scientific method, proved correct. For astrologers there were no surprises. For centuries, these celestial bodies were seen as being linked to certain temperaments (see also Ertel, 1990; Gauquelin and Tracz, 1990; Ertel, 1993; Gauquelin, F., 1995).

What Gauquelin called hypothesis of character (or personality) traits had actually already been suggested since astrology began to take a more psychological slant and move away from the fatalistic interpretations.

Heredity

Gauquelin tested the possibility of similarities between parents and children, as suggested by Kepler some centuries ago, but found nothing. Then he thought of a planetary heredity motivated by the results he had obtained with the professions. He wanted to show that children tend to be born under the same planetary patterns as their parents, and found significant results for the Moon, Mars, Jupiter and Saturn, as in previous experiments, and also for Venus.

Gauquelin stated his hypothesis: "When at the birth of a parent (father or mother), a specific planet was in one of the two zones, rising or culmination, the child should preferably also come into the world when that same planet is near rising or culmination. And, conversely, when, at the parents' birth, the planet was outside of both those zones, then often this would also happen with the children."

Using the birth data of more than 30,000 parents and children, he confirmed that children have a tendency to be born at the time a given planet, positioned at the rising or upper culmination, also occupied that same region of space at the birth of their parents. The similarities were valid for both the father and the mother. If both were born with the same planet in zones one and four, the tendency for the child to follow this pattern doubled. Eleven years later, Gauquelin again repeated the experiment and again obtained significant results. There were no significant correlations found for Mercury, Uranus, Neptune, Pluto and the Sun.

Finally, Gauquelin found that this planetary heredity effect was not manifested when the child was born of cesarean birth, or if the birth was medically induced.

Unfortunately, when in 1984 the Gauquelin couple and five collaborators repeated the experiment of heredity, this time using an even bigger sample, the result was insignificant, casting doubt on the validity of the phenomenon. In early 1990, however, Italian astrologer Ciro Discepolo obtained encouraging results with more than 75,000 samples, correlating the solar cosmosign of the father and mother with the Ascendant cosmosign of the son or daughter (Barbault, A., n/d; Discelo, C., and Miele, L., n/d)). The study was done in collaboration with the Department of Mathematics and Statistics of the University of Naples.

The Difficult Dialogue with Science

However, scientists did not recognize Gauquelin's results even though he conducted the research according to academic standards. But Gauquelin persisted. Statistician Jean Porte examined the data and, while not accepting the "astral influence," acknowledged the validity of the work and said he found no errors. After that, Jean Dath of the Belgian Committee for the Scientific Study of Alleged Paranormal Phenomena said the same about Gauquelin's statistical method, but along with his peers was not convinced that it could be true.

Five years later, Gauquelin again contacted the Belgian Committee and proposed to reproduce the experiment with a new group of Belgian and French sports champions. He expected, as at other times, a significantly higher frequency of Mars in the key sectors. The committee accepted and conducted the survey under the conditions proposed by Gauquelin. The result was positive. The sample of 535 champions confirmed the previous observations (see Figure 5.8). Discussions dragged on and the results were not published. Professor Koenigsfeld, chairman of the Committee, wrote to a fellow researcher: "In fact, we checked the calculations of Mr. Gauquelin and agreed with them. . . . But we do not agree with his conclusions, we cannot accept them."

It was not all disappointment,

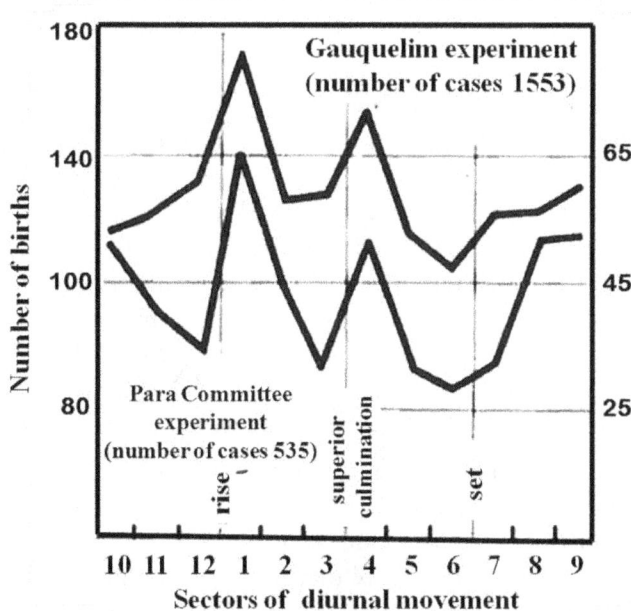

Figure 5.8 Sample of the Belgian Committee.

though. In 1975, none other than the psychologist Hans Eysenck, from the University of London, praised the work of Gauquelin: "I think it may be said that, as far as objectivity of observation, statistical significance of differences, verification of the hypothesis, and replicability are concerned, there are few sets of data in psychology which could compete with these observations." In 1976 the two submitted a paper to the XXI International Congress of Psychology, headquartered in Paris, but the work was not accepted.

The same year *The Humanist* published the authoritarian and dogmatic anti-astrology manifesto signed by 186 scientists, some of which, when later interviewed by the BBC, acknowledged that they knew nothing about astrology. The same magazine published an article by Jerome Lawrence, in which he sharply criticized the work of Gauquelin. Gauquelin later responded to the criticisms of Jerome, and the statistician Marvin Zelen proposed an experiment to verify the validity of the Mars Effect (Zelen, 1976) to either corroborate or invalidate it, "without ambiguity" and "objectively." Gauquelin accepted, the test was done and once again the result confirmed the results. After this, Paul Kurtz, editor of *The Humanist*, Zelen and astronomer George Abell wrote an article that cleverly manipulated the data and also questioned the honesty of Gauquelin (Zelen, Kurtz and Abell, 1977). Elizabeth L. Scott, professor of statistics at Berkeley, wrote a note to the magazine criticizing the errors of the article. The note was never published.

Michel Gauquelin did not prove that astrology works, as some astrologers wish, or that it does not work, as skeptics say. His experiments are important for astrology, and can contribute to the development of more work in this area, including the development of syntactically oriented methods for chart reading and a thorough revision of what the correlation between the astrological chart and personality differences really means.

In 1976, Paul Kurtz announced the creation of the Committee for the Scientific Investigation of Claims of the Paranormal (CSICOP), which had absolutely nothing to do with science. It was just a group of individuals, mostly males, who were against the paranormal, religion, astrology, esotericism, and mysticism, everything that was not scientific orthodoxy. And to prove that they were right and undisputedly in possession of the truth, they would do almost anything. Paul Kurtz had no qualms about resorting to activities that were completely contrary to the protocol of the scientific method to defeat Gauquelin. One of his most ridiculous and deplorable episodes is known as The sTARBABY Case, which is presented in Chapter 6. Interestingly, the (pseudo) skeptics do not tell this story when they decide to angrily lash astrology. They conveniently step widely around this episode and many others that certainly would cause embarrassment, even among his admirers.

Another very badly told story about the alleged invalidation of the so-ealled Mars Effect by the Comité Français pour l'Étude des Phenomenes Paranormaux (French Committee for the Study of Paranormal Phenomena), or CFEPP, caused euphoria in organizations and conferences of pseudo-skeptics. It began after a controversial article by Michel Rouzé that was published in 1981 in the French magazine Science et Vie. In it he stated that after 20 years, research leaves no doubt as to the inexistence of the Mars Effect. A baseless assertion. Gauquelin wrote a response, but the editor, a member of CFEPP, declined to publish it and proposed a study to try to resolve the issue. Gauquelin accepted the suggestion and presented the procedures to be performed for the experiment, as he had on previous occasions, pointing out the conditions under which the Mars Effect appears. More than a year later he received the response from CFEPP, and in the October 1982 issue of Science et Vie the protocol was published that would guide the experiment; the protocol was mutually agreed upon by Gauquelin and CFEPP.

There were two important conditions for the emergence of the Mars Effect: natural birth (prior to 1950) and eminence. Thus, athletes would have to be the most eminent in their categories. Another condition agreed upon was that the CFEPP should pass on to Gauquelin all information relating to the stages of the experiment as they were conducted. However, the data collection ended in April 1986 and Gauquelin only heard news from CFEPP in a preliminary report he received in October 1990, i.e., eight years after establishing the agreement. Three items of the protocol had been violated, including the obligation to keep Gauquelin up to date with the research development.

Dr. Suitbert Ertel (Ertel and Irving, 1996) said that between December 23 and 25, 1994, at the Sixth European Skeptics Congress in Oostende, Belgium, the results of research done by CFEPP were presented, demolishing the Mars Effect. The so-called research was hailed by part of the press as the final blow against the claims of Gauquelin, and by extension the victory of science (i.e., scientificism) over astrology. The histrionic CSICOP even published a book on the subject (Benski, C. et al., 1996). This was countered by Suitbert Ertel, professor of psychology at the Georg-Elias-Muller-Institut fur Psychologie, and one of the most knowledgeable of the history and technical details surrounding the Mars Effect. In *The Tenacious Mars Effect*, Ertel clearly demonstrates that the analysis made by CFEPP is biased; that the sample containing the data is also biased; that the committee ignored basic rules of scientific procedure; and that the results still support the validity of the Mars effect.

CFEPP's decisions, such as the inclusion of non-eminent athletes and the non-use of eminent athletes, for whom there was data that was known to the committee, constituted another clear violation of the protocol signed between both parties. Moreover, the choice of 12 sectors instead of 36, the division now considered more appropriate to identify the Mars Effect, according to Gauquelin, also made a difference. The level of expectancy, i.e., the frequency of birth occurring at random, used by CFEEP was very high: 18.2 percent, exceeding all calculations made before. And it's with this value that we compare the observed frequencies. Interestingly, there was absolutely no comment on this anomalous result. Despite all this, Ertel shows that the Mars Effect appears in the CFEPP sample. Taking into account that this effect depends on the degree of eminence, Ertel divided the sample into sub-samples differentiated by degree of eminence. With this he hoped to obtain higher frequencies in the sub-samples of the most prominent athletes, varying towards less in the sub-samples of athletes of lesser projection. The criterion used for eminence was the number of citations, i.e., the number of sources in which the athlete is named.

In Figure 5.9 (see page 94), a part of the sample (N = 585), which includes only athletes of the four categories most represented (soccer, athletics, cycling and rugby) is divided into three levels of eminence, shown on the abscissa axis; in the axis of the ordinates, the frequency as a percentage with which Mars occupies the key sectors, is marked as G sectors, so G percentage. The frequencies in G increase with increasing eminence, which once again proves the thesis of Gauquelin.

So once again Gauquelin was deceived, and he believed those he should not have believed in. Gauquelin found almost no interlocutors in academia; therefore, any organization or institution that wanted to assess his experiments was welcome. After all, he was a scientist and needed the backing of his peers. But unfortunately those who agreed to assess the Mars Effect did so with the sordid intention of merely discrediting him, even though they had to resort to devious methods to do so. And that was precisely what happened. One of the pearls of Benski's conclusion in

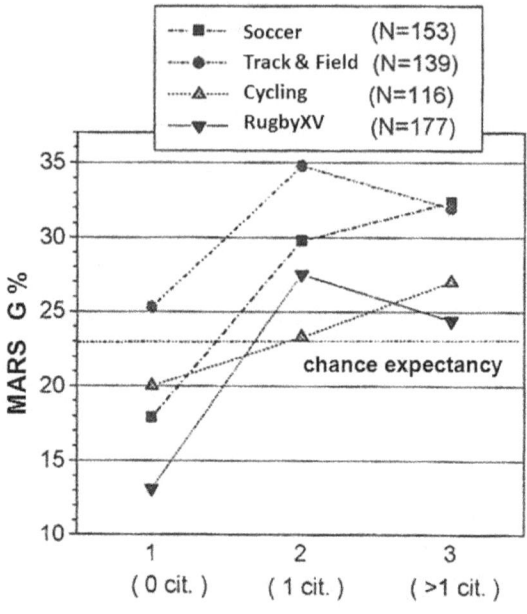

Figure 5.9 Frequency of Mars in the Key Sectors According to eminence.

his book is a reference to his own findings as "definitive." A scientist who has the arrogance to claim that his research is definitive is not a scientist.

In Benski's book, Dr. Nienhuys, who followed the work of CFEPP, makes discrediting comments on the criticisms of Dr. Ertel. In his response (Ertel, Suitbert, n/d), however, in which once again he demonstrates the correlation between the Mars Effect and the eminence of the athletes, Ertel ends up touching on a very important and enlightening point. Asking himself who would be responsible for the posture assumed by the French committee, he arrives at the unsurprising name of the ubiquitous chairman of CSICOP, Paul Kurtz, always present and active when it comes to discredit astrology. It was this man who promoted the CFEPP study. Moreover, no investigation or research on astrology that includes the participation of Kurtz can be considered reliable.

Geoffrey Dean, a former astrologer who joined the ranks of scientificist fundamentalism, asserted that the times of birth used in the Gauquelin research, obviously provided by parents to the birth record offices, were false. Because of the belief they had in astrology, these parents invented fictitious times so the planets would be close to the angles and their descendants would believe that they could one day become famous.

In his last book, *Neo-Astrology: the Copernican Revolution*, published in 1991, Gauquelin abandons the ambiguous, sometimes even hostile, position that he held in relation to astrology and recognizes himself as a neo-astrologer. Disenchanted with the prejudices and the manipulations of the organized skeptics, he now seems to see things more clearly. If on the one hand the results of his experiments do reject most of what we know as astrology, on the other he perceives the irrational motivations of a part of the scientific community that aggressively repels anything that does not confirm its own ideology.

The work of Michel Gauquelin is a saga of more than 40 years. Gauquelin faced the prejudice of both the academic community, for obvious reasons, and from part of the astrological community because of a lack of scientific training, and a vision blurred by magic, occultism and esotericism. If on many occasions he misread astrology, he should not be blamed for this. Astrologers repeated the echoes of tradition with no regard for a necessary critical view. Astrology seemed a dinosaur out of time, insisting on an archaic terminology and on mythical and magical thinking without worrying about scientific method.

Gauquelin did not prove that astrology works, as some astrologers desire, or that it does not work, as skeptics desire. It is very common to come across biased and superficial readings of the works of this great researcher. The biases seem to feed rigid positions on both sides. We must, therefore, be careful. His experiments are very important for astrology, once they are properly scrutinized and analyzed, and so they contribute to the development of more judicious works. The development of syntactically oriented methods for reading, and a thorough revision of what the correlation between the astrological chart and personality differences really means are urgent tasks, without which one cannot understand the astrological phenomenon or even design new experiments with appropriate scientific rigor.

Other Research

Many of the experiments conducted with the intention to evaluate astrology have lost their *raison d'etre* because they were directed at a non-existent or, at best, confused target. Astrology is not exactly a divinatory art, nor are its signs proper representations of worldly things. Astrological symbolism points to the representational universe of the human mind itself, its emotions and cognitive orientations. Hence, one can deduce personality traits from the symbolic dynamics of an astrological chart. This does not imply the existence of a predestined fate in celestial mechanics or the possibility of mapping the concrete relationship between the individual and external reality. The astrological chart is a representation of subjective reality through symbols that appear to be associated with different structures or to the different aspects of personality. It is therefore a representation of a representation, i.e., it reveals a signical process that occurs in the mind.

Since the first Gauquelin experiments in the 1950s to the present day, a few attempts have been made to assess astrology, whether as a tool to analyze the personality or as a tool for predicting future events or identifying something in the past. We have seen that there seems to be a big mistake, both on the part of many astrologers, as on the part of skeptics in relation to the supposed nature of the astrological phenomenon. What can be interpreted or decoded in an astrological chart? Certainly not events of the outside world. Hence the impossibility of identifying, for example, the profession of a person or his or her experiences. There are no patterns in the chart that are associated with this or that professional activity. Often, however, astrologers were tested for this capacity. They believed they could do it, according to a tradition they never dared to question. Unfortunately, astrologers have been accomplices in some embarrassing situations in which neither party, astrologers and scientists, seemed to know what they were doing.

We therefore have to disregard all the experiments conducted to evaluate the alleged capacity of astrology to predict an individual's profession. Such a feat is simply not possible. Even taking into account the reading of a chart as a whole, nothing in the chart points toward a profession or any kind of social role. There is no direct relationship between planets or cosmosigns and professions. The insistence on this untenable and unrealistic idea only exposes astrology to ridicule. For the sake of astrology, that illusion, at least in part, has been abandoned by contemporary astrologers. Astrology also lacks the power to distinguish the chart of a violent killer from that of an apparently peaceful citizen, as Gauquelin wanted to assess; but it can, indeed, identify, for example, a level of aggressiveness. Most aggressive or violent people, however, do not commit murders because of fear of punishment, lack of opportunity or venting their aggression by playing sports, working in the police or armed forces, in verbal discussions, in sex, or in other ways that do not involve criminal activity.

Correlations with the Position of the Sun

In an experiment carried out by Silverman (Silverman, B.I., 1971), the objective was to assess whether there are personality differences in people born in each of the twelve signs. For this, he used the Rokeach Value Survey, a questionnaire that assesses the system of social values, i.e., values that the individual deems important and the personality descriptions related to Sun signs found in four astrology books. Based on these descriptions, Silverman determined that in the value Equality, those born under the signs of Libra and Aquarius should have a higher score than the others; in the value Honesty, Sagittarius should predominate; in Helpfulness, Pisces and Aquarius; in Family Security, Taurus and Cancer; and in the value Intellectuality, Virgo, Gemini and Capricorn. The results were all negative and the author concluded that "the position of the Sun at birth does not serve to predict an individual personality."

While personality traits and behavioral predispositions are innate and biologically determined, at least in large part, value systems are the result of social conditioning. This is not what astrology deals with. Among the values chosen by Silverman, some could be influenced by personality traits, while others such as Equality and Intellectuality give rise to some doubts in this regard. Even so, the attributions are poor.

For example, the typical Aquarian personality (which is not the same as having Aquarius as a Sun sign) seeks distinction, is strongly attracted to the unconventional, wants to be different from the average, rejects being dominated and is moderately dominating. How can someone who wants to stand out from others think about equality? Differentiation is one of the key words to understand the meaning of the Aquarius and, more importantly, the Leo-Aquarius axis. Equal opportunity for all? Aquarius would say yes, provided that he or she is not equal to others. Fraternity? It is a value that is associated with Pisces and not with Aquarius, as is erroneously thought, because first of all it presupposes a high emotional charge.

Helpfulness also does not concern Aquarius, but Virgo and Pisces. The value of the family is emphasized in Cancer, but is not something that characterizes Taurus. As for intellectuality, we understand that the various interests that we could call intellectual are distributed among all cosmosigns. The attributions, as we can see, are not correct, whether by almost total lack of knowledge and experience in astrology or becasue of flaws in traditional astrology. Having read descriptions of the Sun signs does not mean you are knowledgeable in astrology, something the author notes in the article. His hypothesis regarding compatibility between the signs for love relationships is childish. He knows nothing about synastry. We cannot blame him, however, if his sources misinformed him.

We have also seen that personality traits or factors that involve interpersonal relationships, at least in some of their sub-factors or facets, are much more related to the rising cosmosign than to the solar cosmosign, which by itself invalidates this type of evaluation. It is much easier to do a survey of the Sun sign than to verify the Ascendant and planets in contact with this sector of the chart. I have analyzed the subtle differences between the personality indicators (Sun, Moon, Ascendant, Mercury, Venus and Mars) and pointed out the difficulties in devising an experiment that can accurately assess the appropriate signifier in terms of personality structure or aspect. This criticism, as well as others, applies to many other studies exalted by the skeptics as evidence that astrology does not work.

When an astrologer interprets a horoscope, the solar sign should be treated as a component of a greater and systemic whole. By simply adding up the parts, the mechanistic researcher will not get the whole as a result. Therefore, it is important to understand how the logic of an astrological chart works.

An astrologer should analyze the chart as a whole, not just the individual components. Understanding this principle is essential in order to correctly interpret a chart. It is no less important to design an experiment that, in fact, takes into consideration the complexity of astrological dynamics.

Experiments that used only the Sun sign as an indicator mostly had negative results. Besides the work of Silverman, Pellegrini (1973) attempted to investigate the possible relationship between Sun signs and individual differences. He used the California Psychological Inventory (CPI) for this, a test that measures several personality traits involved in interpersonal behavior. The test was conducted with 288 students (no information on age). The variable Sun sign was significant in only four scales of the test: Communality, Socialization, Flexibility, and Femininity, although the result was significant only in Femininity, highlighting the following cosmosigns: Capricorn, Sagittarius, Libra, Leo, Scorpio and Virgo. The traits with high scores in Femininity are appreciative, patient, helpful, gentle, moderate, persevering, sincere, accepting of others, conscientious, and sympathetic. There are, however, no features common to these six cosmosigns. The correlation was not confirmed by other studies (Tyson, G.A., 1977).

Veno and Pamment (1979) used the Eysenck Personality Inventory (EPI) on 692 college students and calculated the Extraversion and Neuroticism (emotional instability) scores. The goal was to determine, first, whether those born with the Sun in fire and air cosmosigns were more likely to be extraverts, and whether those born in earth and water signs would have lower scores on this factor; and, second, whether if those born with the Sun in a water cosmosign would have higher scores in Neuroticism. Again there was no correlation between the measures tested and the Sun signs. Another similar study with students (Saklofske, D.H. et al., 1982) also showed negative results. Jackson and Fiebert (1980) also used the EPI on 174 subjects in order to measure the Extraversion-Introversion dimension, and did not obtain significant correlations. Russell and Wagstaff (1983), also with the EPI, found no relationship between these factors and the Sun sign in a sample of 350 individuals. These authors also added the positions of the Moon, Mercury and Venus, concluding there was no indication that sustained the astrological correlations. In a study conducted in Brazil (Rodrigues, P.R.G., 1997) with 275 subjects, relating Sun signs to scores on the 16PF Cattel scales, no statistically significant results were obtained, but some differences point to what would be expected in an astrological pattern.

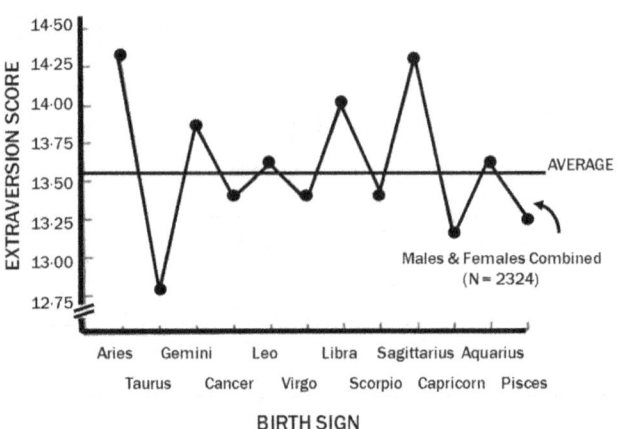

Figure 5.10 Extraversion Score According to the Birth Sun Sign.

The studies of Veno and Pamment, Saklofske, Jackson and Fiebert, and of Russell and Wagstaff were certainly a reaction to an article written by Mayo, White and Eysenck, published in 1978 in the *Journal of Social Psychology*. In this work the authors tested the hypothesis that the odd numbered zodiacal signs (fire and air) are related to Extraversion, and even numbered signs (earth and water) to Introversion. They also verified another hypothesis: that people born with the Sun in the water element signs tend to be more emotional. The EPI was applied to 917 adult males and 1,407 females, a total of 2,324 subjects, to measure the dimensions of Extraversion and Neuroticism, a sample size that could be more revealing than the subsequent ones. For the Extraversion factor, the result was a pattern in which the fire and air signs scored above average in the EPI, and earth and water scored below average. Figure 5.10 shows these measurements.

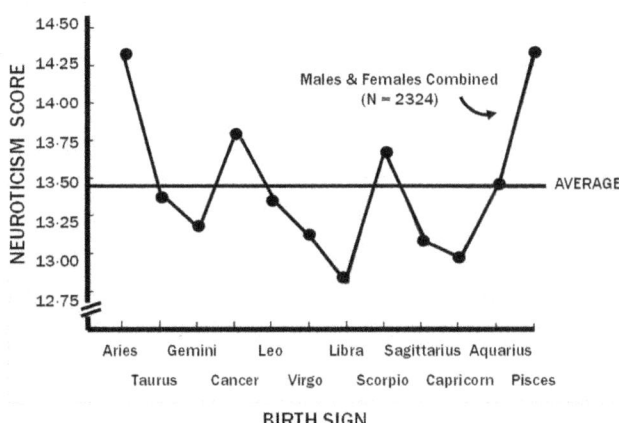

Figure 5.11 Neuroticism Score According to the Birth Sun Sign.

The same procedure with regard to measurements of Neuroticism compared to the Sun sign showed the three water signs (Cancer, Scorpio and Pisces) and also Aries, a fire sign, with scores above average in this personality dimension that corresponds to emotional instability-emotional stability (see Figure 5.11).

Smithers and Cooper (1978) found similar results using 559 college students also submitted to the EPI; Jackson (1979) also managed to reproduce in New Zealand the pattern obtained by Mayo for Extraversion, but not for the Neuroticism factor. Then, in Holland, van Rooij, Brak and Commandeur (1988) also replicated the experiment with success in 992 subjects, but this time with less significant results. The Dutch study only investigated the Extraversion factor.

Two hypotheses have been suggested to explain the discrepancy between the studies apparently favorable to astrology and those that were unfavorable. The first was presented by Eysenck, who participated in the work of Mayo, and defends the idea that auto-attribution was the factor responsible for the "distortion" in the result, i.e., people who know the characteristics of their Sun sign, and accept them, begin to consider them as valid for describing their own personality. Even after dividing the sample into two groups, those who knew something of astrology and those who do not, Eysenck (1984) was not satisfied. He replicated the experiment with 122 adults, divided the sample into three groups (those who were familiar with astrology, those who were unfamiliar and the uncertain) and "demonstrated" that people versed in astrology get a higher correlation, followed by those who are uncertain and finally those who say they know nothing of astrology. So does the auto-attribution explain Mayo's results? Without providing greater details, Eysenck cites a replication of the original experiment by Mayo with 2,274 people. The sample was divided into three groups: those who knew a lot, those who knew little and those who knew nothing of astrology. Those who answered correctly more often were those who knew little, followed by those who knew nothing and finally those who knew a lot. Eysenck explains the strange result by saying that those who knew a lot took into account other astrological indications of their map to make it auto-attributable, like the Moon, the Ascendant, etc., thereby reducing the importance of the Sun, which for those who knew little would be absolute. For Eysenck, those who knew nothing actually knew a little and therefore "contaminated" the sample. My opinion is that Eysenck's *ad hoc* explanations tried to make results fit into conventional models.

The other hypothesis, more simple and sensible, ponders that the Mayo study only managed to detect an isolated astrological factor. Astrology personality traits emerge from a network of interacting variables, and not from the nature of a single variable, especially if one considers that extraversion is expressed mainly by the Ascendant (see also van Rooij, 1988; Smithers and Cooper, 1978).

Another attempt to correlate the Sun signs to each of the MMPI (Minnesota Multiphasic Personality Inventory) scales came to the conclusion that there is no evidence in favor of the "folklore" concepts of astrology (Dahlstrom, W.G. et al., 1996). The MMPI assesses mental health, and it is clear that there is no correlation between certain mental disorders and the Sun sign.

In the late 1990s, French astrologer Didier Castille developed an interesting study on marriage, using 6,498,320 marriages. The zodiacal longitudes of the Sun for each spouse were compared and the number of marriages in which the distance between the solar positions was around 30 or fewer degrees was well above random. This means there is a clear tendency of men and women with the same Sun sign to marry. The results with Mercury and Venus were also positive, although among the lunar longitudes there was no significant correlation.

Position of the Sun and Other Indicators

In an article published in 1974 by the *Journal of Psychology*, Silverman and Whitmer, using a small sample of 130 subjects, including students and staff of Stockton State College, concluded that the descriptions of the Ascendant, Sun and Moon signs do not serve as indicators of personality when compared to the self-assessments of these subjects and the assessment made by a friend of each. As this is a study that includes not just the Sun but the Moon and Ascendant, apparently it should cover the minimum number of variables for an astrological analysis of temperament. In fact, these three astrological indicators would be sufficient for a basic characterization. But it was not the case.

The first mistake was in obtaining the time of birth. Participants were asked to provide the exact time and location of birth. Those who did not know were asked to ask their parents. However, this procedure is flawed, because this information is not generally known, not even by the mother, who often has only a vague recollection of the time the child was born, or at best, recalls an approximate time. The only reliable source is the birth certificate. For personality analysis, an error of a few minutes can be tolerated as long as the moment of birth is not very close to a change of Ascendant sign. As we have seen, contiguous signs are quite dissimilar, i.e., their traits are not correlated. This type of error inserts data which distorts the analysis, thus invalidating it.

The experimenters attributed to each zodiac sign a value on a five-point scale applied on eight personality dimensions. After calculating the Sun, Moon and Ascendant signs for each subject, they took the average of these values for each dimension. Therefore, everyone had a value that corresponded to a specific dimension of personality. Besides the problem of the birth time, ignoring the differences between the three astrological indicators (Sun, Moon and Ascendant) in relation to each specific dimension and taking an average was another error that invalidates the study.

Clarke, Gabriels and Barnes (1996) tested the hypothesis that people with the Sun, Moon or Ascendant occupying a positive sign (fire and air) would be more extraverted than those in which Sun, Moon and Ascendant were in negative signs (earth and water). They also tested the hypothesis of emotionality-water sign. There were 190 participants, all first-year students of psychology, with whom he carried out the EPI. For Extraversion, it was found that the difference in scores between positive and negative signs was very small, although higher for the first, except in the case of the Ascendant. The only significant result was when both the Sun and the Moon occupied positive signs. As for the relationship of emotionality-water signs, none of the differences was significant.

In turn, the study by Hartmann, Reuter and Nyborg (2006), with two samples totaling about 15,000 individuals, found no correlation between solar signs and individual differences in personality. Here, however, the dimensions of personality, based on Eysenck's model, were derived from results obtained with the MMPI-II, a test for mental illness, which I believe brings into question the applicability of the result in the validation of descriptions of the solar sign.

Global Reading Evaluation of the Astrological Chart

Among the first trials to assess the ability of astrologers to correctly associate the astrological chart with profession, life history, intelligence and personality traits were the three studies conducted by Vernon Clark in the 1960s (Eysenck and Nias, 1984). These pioneering experiments showed results that were reasonably favorable toward astrology, and all were devised by astrologers.

Other tests (Carlson, S., 1985, McGrew and McFall, 1990 and 1992, Nanninga, R. 1996/97), had the same goal and with more or less similar methods and sought to test astrologers regarding attribution of personality-temperament and events occurring in a person's life. The results were apparently disappointing for astrology and its claims. The first study was published in *Nature*, the second by the *Journal of Scientific Exploration*, and in an extended version by *Correlation*, which also published the last one.

The conditions of these tests were arranged with astrologers who accepted them, judging them reasonable and fair. Studies of isolated factors have always been criticized by the astrological community because they were not testing astrology as it is practiced in a daily basis. Still, part of the problem is the astrologers themselves and their lack of method, the use of questionable techniques, the belief that they can predict future events and their lack of familiarity with scientific research. They end up accepting the conditions and the planning of an experiment without really knowing what they are accepting. The pseudo-skeptics set up perfect traps to ensnare them and "prove" that astrology is a great illusion. It is naive to think that they want to test the validity of astrology as they already have a strong and deep-seated opinion that astrology is a superstition. Therefore, the experiment will serve only to confirm their hypothesis.

Describing Carlson's experiment in a simple manner, 83 volunteers were chosen for the test group and 94 for the control group. The experiment was divided into two parts. In the first part, the volunteers had their birth chart calculated and interpreted by participating astrologers. Each subject had to select among three interpretations that they deemed to be theirs. The other two were interpretations of charts of other individuals in the group. Both in the test group, as in the control group, the choice of correct interpretation was close to what was expected at a random level. In the second part, each astrologer received the birth chart of one volunteer and three personality questionnaires (CPI), duly completed, one of which belonged to the same person as that of the chart and the other two belonged to other volunteers. The astrologer should then choose the CPI that best described the personality type of the chart. Once again, the performance of the two groups, control and test, was close to a level expected by chance. Still revered by CSICOP as one of the "best scientific studies on astrology," its flaws are obvious. In the first part, the question being raised is the possibility that the subject distinguishes from three personality descriptions the one that is his or hers. The volunteers were unable to select their CPI profile from two others, which therefore invalidates the CPI as a reliable test. However, if the CPI is not a reliable test, then the second part of the experiment makes no sense. Eysenck himself criticized the absence of an experienced psychologist to apply the personality test and prepare the experiment, and also the quality of the test itself (the CPI). And Carlson was a newly graduated in *physics*! Why is it that *Nature* has allowed such a poor and ridiculous paper to blemish the credibility of its pages?

The experiment by McGrew and McFall is much clearer. The authors, in agreement with an American astrological organization, received a list drawn up by astrologers of 61 questions of a personal nature. The volunteer subjects provided their birth data without knowing that this was a study on astrology. Besides this information, the volunteers responded to questionnaires from two psychological tests and were also photographed. Six astrologers and one control participated in the study. Having on one hand the answers to questions, the results of psychological tests and two pictures of each volunteer, and on the other the astrological charts, their task was to correctly pair information and charts. The result was disappointing. Again the astrologers failed to perform well.

Another test sponsored by an association of skeptics, The Skepsis Foundation, was similar to that of McGrew and McFall. The astrologers were given the birth data of seven people and seven completed questionnaires. The goal was to find the correspondence between the charts and the questionnaires. Again, the performance of the astrologers was disappointing, nothing more than chance.

A Solution to a Dilemma

Could this be a confirmation that astrology is a great illusion, that when faced with scientific assessments its claims prove to be false? Or as some astrologers wish, scientific methods are inadequate to validate astrology because of the nature of this knowledge system? Who is right? I believe that none of the parties is correct. Both are wrong in their desire to protect their positions and do not see what they do not want to see.

Basically, two problems must be solved. The first concerns the techniques used by astrologers, many of them useless or, when effective, poorly applied, that is, without method. The "free" reading that has been taught to astrology students is completely unacceptable. When combined with confusing interpretations inspired by Jungian analysis, results are vague, imprecise and hazy. To further worsen the situation, many astrologers believe they can predict events, a highly dubious belief. In the three aforementioned tests, astrologers included questions about religious beliefs, current profession and previous occupations, honesty, height, weight, color of skin, hair and eyes, relationships with parents and siblings, educational level and occupation of parents, neighborhood and other issues.

An example of an unreliable although widely used technique is the counting of planets above and below the horizon and to the east and west of the meridian as an indicator of extraversion-introversion. The variables used are so numerous that anything can be found on the chart, which is the same as saying that nothing can be found. When the astrologer has the chart of someone totally unknown to him or her and with whom he or she cannot talk, it is extremely difficult to make an objective analysis because of the huge amount of variables. As the astrologer is busy interpreting exotic configurations and deciphering the occurrence of psychological complexes of a psychoanalytical nature, he or she moves beyond that hard core where the basic and essential information can be found. Just a careful reading of these few variables is enough to be able to extract from the chart what it actually has to offer. That done, possible extrapolations can be made, which are the behavioral tendencies of the individual.

The second problem is less obvious. It consists of comparing the profile that emerges from a personality test to the interpretation of a birth chart. At first it seems a good idea but for the fact that these are two very different tools, especially in regards of the conceptual level. The Extraversion dimension, for example, is a construct formed from a set of personality traits that have a certain level of correlation. These same features must be properly identified in the systemic dynamics of the astrological chart; otherwise the comparison is not valid. Moreover, the test was standardized, i.e., the score obtained refers to the performance of testing in relation to the distribution of scores in a group taken as reference. In this case, the concept of extraversion is, in every sense, operational. It is a graduated scale. Astrology also needs to work with operational concepts, and start to use a well-defined syntax and a set of reading instructions, i.e., an algorithm that can be used in the same way by all those who wish to interpret a chart.

To try to identify the measure of a personality trait, or even a personality factor, with the position of the Sun, Moon, or Ascendant in a particular zodiac sign has been a gross error in the very common practice of some researchers who eagerly want to refute the validity of astrological phenomenon, but have little concern in studying how the dynamics of an astrological chart as a structured system works. If they did, they would notice that a personality trait can only be inferred from a network of interacting astrological variables. The trait or sub-factor of aggression, for example, is not defined in astrology by the isolated position of the Sun, Moon or any planet. Not even just by the configuration of the Ascendant, which would be the best starting point for characterizing the level of effective social aggressiveness of a person in astrological terms. In the bibliography of scientific articles on astrology, it is interesting and sad to observe the almost absence of actual astrological references, if not their total absence. The researcher simply does not know how the astrological model is used, has only a vague and distant notion of what astrology is, no more than this. Not knowing anything, or almost nothing about that which he/she proposes to refute, he/she is left only with warping or misrepresenting their object of "study" in order to facilitate the invalidation. Frequently, these scientists are motivated by an emotional discomfort for certain alternative worldviews, which leads them to fight "superstition," that they imagine threatens the prestige of their status quo.

The Barnum Effect and Auto-Attribution

Ever since the famous article by Forer in 1949 about the fallacy of personal validation, or Barnum Effect, skeptics cling to this argument to show that the descriptions of psychological profiles made by astrologers are false and rely on the gullibility of people. Skeptics say these descriptions are so vague and general that they apply to anyone, and therefore would be validated by the astrologer's client as legitimate and relevant. In the 1960s, when Gauquelin struggled to be taken seriously by a scientific community that showed him nothing but contempt, he published an advertisement in a newspaper without revealing his real name and offered to send a free personalized horoscope to those who wrote him to request the service. In the advertisement he asked for the name, address, date and place of birth. There was, however, no individual horoscope, but a single text that was dispatched to all indiscriminately. He said that 94 percent of those who responded to the offer stated that they recognized the text as a description of their own personality (Gauquelin, 1979).

This is an example of the Barnum Effect. The referred text was an astrological "analysis" generated by a computer program and sold by a company called Ordinamus. Gauquelin requested one using a false name and the address of another person. With the intention to "test" astrology, he provided as his personal data the date of birth of Marcel Petiot, a terrible criminal who had cruelly killed more than sixty people. The description from the program, however, gave no indication about the sadistic and violent Petiot character, nor that he could potentially be a criminal. With this electronic caricature of astrological chart interpretation, which does not even take into account the Ascendant, Gauquelin intended to invalidate the astrology judiciously practiced by serious astrologers, that in no way resembles the probably simplistic algorithms used in the program. But these little tricks had no effect on his being accepted by the skeptics. Later Gauquelin had bitter experiences with these gentlemen and would better understand the meaning of the word fraud.

The distribution in the general population of the variation of different personality traits can be expressed by a normal curve. This means that the majority occupy a position near the midpoint of any scale that serves to measure a trait, whatever it may be: aggressiveness, dominance, responsibility, creativity or affectiveness. It is therefore natural that a typical description of a cosmosign makes no reference to extreme characteristics, but presents the typical profile of an average person, someone who is neither introverted nor extraverted, emotionally balanced or unbalanced, aggressive or indifferent, etc. The Barnum Effect is not so much the result of a supposed naivety but the readiness in acknowledging a lot of our own personality in generic descriptions (Hampson, Gilmour & Harris, 1978). Even in good quality astrological analysis, there are common phrases that might as well describe psychological aspects of the majority of the population. We are analyzing human beings, and despite individual differences, humans have more similarities than dissimilarities. Some scientists, however, feel a certain pleasure in calling the layman, at best, naive.

Skeptics also cite popular publications that describe in simplistic and often misleading terms the zodiac signs and presuppose the existence of twelve personality types, as well as identify the person with their Sun sign—something like "you are your sign"! An example is the books by the late Linda Goodman, an American author whose books are sold worldwide and regarded as astrological literature (Snyder, C.R., 1974). It takes a lot of good will to call Goodman's texts astrology. Nevertheless, the skeptic builds his argument around this folklore disastrology, saying that its validation by so many people is pure Barnum Effect.

We have seen that the results of experiments aimed to test the correlation between the personality traits and the characteristics of people's Sun sign are ambiguous. When the result is not in favor of astrology, skeptics are quick to rejoice and say that this is an important piece of evidence contrary to the astrologer's claims. But if the experiment is in favor of astrology, the explanation is auto-attribution, i.e., many people internalize the descriptions of their Sun sign and naively believe they are made up of those features. Even worse, they start behaving according to the model of their zodiac sign. It's as if astrology induces people to be different from themselves. Can this be true? Does astrology have the power to transform an introvert into an extravert? An insensitive guy into a sentimental man? If that really happens, even the standardizing of personality tests must be infected by the belief in astrology, as a large number of people know the characteristics that make up their Sun sign. And what about genetic determinations? Will they be outweighed by the "naivety" of people? Frankly, I think it very unlikely.

In fact, some studies (Wunder, 2003) found evidence that not knowing the birth solar sign characteristics made the correlations between the sign and the measure of certain personality dimensions vanish. But this does not always happen, especially in the case of emotional balance measures, such as the dimension of Neuroticism in the EPI inventory (Fourie, 1984), a factor that includes a set of traits more related to the solar and lunar configurations, while extraversion, as pointed out, is more closely related to the configuration of the Ascendant. These are important details that are not adequately addressed in academic studies, almost all of them being superficial, as the researcher usually has a rather superficial and distorted notion of what astrology is. They are more concerned about fulfilling their skeptic's agenda than they are in investigating reality and do not care to delve into the study of what they have allegedly researched.

Time Twins

A topic barely explored by astrological research and which should receive more attention, is that of the births of non-twin children occurring at the same time and in the same city or at very close geographical locations. These are time twins, or astrological twins, because their birth charts are identical or nearly so. What are the similarities that we should expect in these cases? For traditional astrology, as well as personalities and temperaments with very similar characteristics, the twins would show a remarkable timing of facts and events in their lives; for example, marriage, divorce, death of close relatives, surgery, graduation, etc., occurring exactly on the same day or within a range of a few days. The psychological profiles should be expected to be very similar; otherwise there would be no reason to believe in astrology.

In the 1990s Peter Roberts and Helen Greengrass wrote *The Astrology of Time Twins*, which describes the research they did. Project Time Twins, as it was called, obtained data from people born on six dates: December 9, 1934, February 21, 1937, November 14, 1948, July 18, 1950, August 29, 1958 and May 1, 1964. Altogether, 128 people who met the project requirements responded to the researchers' ads. Because the request was for the day of birth, it is clear that for each day there were individuals born at different times, some closer to each other, others more distant. Actually, it was not a legitimate study of time twins. The researchers sought to correlate the difference in the time of birth with differences in measures of personality, other general characteristics and important life events. The result was fairly positive in some respects, such as profession and personality traits, but negative in others, such as events at certain times of life and physical characteristics.

Chapter 6

Skeptics and Pseudo-Skeptics

In a broad sense, skepticism, or a skeptical attitude, is one of doubt and critical thinking in relation to ideas, values and behavior. In the strictest sense, it refers to the rejection of knowledge and the acceptance of only properly demonstrated or demonstrable claims. In short, the skeptic will not accept *a priori* truths. As for pseudo-skepticism, a term that I borrow from the sociologist (and authentic skeptic) Marcello Truzzi, this is a different kind of behavior that can resort to personal insults and attempts to ridicule any claim about the existence of phenomena taken by themselves as "impossible" and whose belief, to a pseudo-skeptic, is motivated by superstition and ignorance. The world is therefore divided between scientific truth and falsehood of everything that is not scientific.

True skepticism has been extremely beneficial to human knowledge. Nothing is better than a skeptical attitude for overcoming prejudices, recognizing manipulation and identifying fantasies. Astrologers should not summarily reject the criticisms made of astrology, or worse, ignore them altogether, assuming that anything goes, nothing is false or is "wrong" with the concepts or techniques that have been used for centuries, just because they have been used for centuries. In virtue of extreme traditionalism and an endemic lack of critical sense, astrology does not correct its mistakes; it continues to foster them.

Answers for the Skeptics

Why does astrology never question its foundations? Unfortunately, many astrologers have difficulty in taking a critical stance in relation to the concepts and techniques of the tradition. In fact, modern astrology is very different from astrology that was practiced in Babylonia and Egypt and also with what was practiced in the Middle Ages. Much was left out, though those who wanted to resurrect the "true" astrology, or the astrology of the past, always kept appearing. They are usually scholars of the history of astrology who become enthusiastic by their research and discoveries, which are indeed important from a historical perspective and have been conducted with great competence. Even so, they rely on an old model, with few innovations. The resistance to self-criticism is immense. We can conclude that astrology as it is practiced today is quite unsatisfactory for the demands of our contemporary Western scientific culture.

Astrology is based on the old geocentric system. Why is the same model still used, now that we know that the universe does not revolve around us? Because it makes no difference to the representation of the sky that we see in an astrological chart, as it is just a reference. This chart is a graphical representation of the sky seen from a specific geographical point at a given moment. If you are on Earth, then it describes the position of the Sun, Moon and planets as they are seen from the Earth, hence the geocentric reference. Indeed, astronomers also use these same geocentric coordinate systems to locate celestial bodies in space. The celestial equator, for example, is nothing but a projection of the terrestrial equator.

Is it not misleading to say that astrology is true only because it has existed for more than three or four thousand years? Yes, of course, this argument is very foolish. It is not the great age of astrology that makes it a valid system of knowledge.

If, when we are born everything is already set and programmed into our lives by the stars, this contradicts everything we know about genetic and socio-cultural influences. This fatalistic view of astrology belongs to the past, and there are very few astrologers who defend this today. So it is not true that contemporary astrology supports this kind of absolute determinism. But on the other hand we still do not know how the correlations of the astrological phenomenon are linked to genetic inheritance, although in both cases the environment controls the expression of any predispositions, whether genotypical or astrological. We see no contradiction of the kind: if the transmission of genetically determined characteristics is true, then astrology should be false, because no event that occurs on Earth is "written in the stars," nor in genes. Behavioral and social events are complex, resulting from the confluence of variables of different levels: phylogenetic, ontogenetic, perinatal, social, cultural, situational, and also astrological, if we consider here the existence of a causal relationship, since the correlation does not necessarily means a relation of cause and effect.

The astrological house systems used by most contemporary Western astrologers are unviable for latitudes closer to the poles. Don't people born in these regions have a birth chart? The Placidus and Koch systems have this limitation. Although not an insurmountable problem, it is one that needs to be resolved. It is likely that the Placidus system is an approximate model, but it works reasonably well. There are others, such as the Equal House system, which does not produce distortions and could be a serious candidate to replace it. One can therefore draw the astrological chart of an inhabitant of Lapland, for example, using this house system.

Astrologers say that signs can match, so if two people with matching signs start a relationship, they will be happy and everything will be all right for them. It seems obvious that in practice this does not work. Of course it does not work. Comparing the solar cosmosign of two people to see if their relationship will work is nonsense. Doing this is just comparing a certain aspect of their personality, or better still, temperament. It is quite another thing to compare astrological charts, with emphasis on the structure of the temperament of each person, so as to infer the degree of compatibility between two people, both in general and with regard to affection. When the synastry of two charts is analyzed, the converging aspects of their temperaments become more obvious as do the likely points of conflict that must be understood and addressed by both if they want to live in relative harmony.

Are horoscope columns in newspapers and online examples of astrology? These horoscopes are not astrology; they really are good for nothing and give a distorted idea of astrology. Their predictions are vague and crude and a pale and dim reflection of what an astrological forecast should be. Moreover, they create embarrassment for astrologers who want to be taken seriously. As entertainment, they may be acceptable and fun, but only in that sense.

There is an astronomical phenomenon called precession of the equinoxes. This movement causes a lag between the constellations of the zodiac and the zodiac signs. When astrologers say, for example, that the Sun is in Capricorn, in fact it should be in Sagittarius, because the difference today is about one whole sign. Thus, all the planetary positions are wrong and astrology is a pack of lies. The biggest mistake here is to confuse the zodiacal constellation with the zodiac sign; these are two distinct concepts. When the Babylonians created the idea of the zodiac, they divided the ecliptic into twelve equal sections (which are the signs of the zodiac) from the vernal equinoctial point, and to each of these sections they gave the name of a constellation. So the constellations were used as a reference and have lent their names to these twelve segments. The aim was to divide the ecliptic into twelve segments of arc that reflected numerically the amount of synodic lunar cycles that occur within one solar cycle or year, i.e., the idea should correspond to the lunar months.

Astrology denies the free will to human beings. So-called free will is a relative condition, as any living being is limited by its own structural or constitutive reality, which does not let you do everything you want, whether with your own body or mind, or in terms of absolute transformation of the environment. There are a number of physical and biological constraints on our actions. A male subject, for example, cannot produce a child within him, as much as he desires this. There is an insurmountable biological obstacle. We believe that from the psychological point of view the astrological correlations generate predispositions, inclinations and tendencies, all of which are rather strong and identifiable in a careful reading of the birth chart. So they do not prevent the expression of our relative free will, as astrology cannot predict the actual, real behavior of an individual, only the regularities that make up the person's pattern of behavior.

The personality descriptions made by an astrologer and their recognition by clients as truly relevant can be explained in that they are so general that they could be used to describe anyone. Unfortunately, part of what is done in psychological astrology can indeed be explained in this way. These descriptions cannot identify a specific personality, or better still, a temperament, and get lost in empty phrases full of clichés. Such "analyses" lack method and therefore fail to reveal anything important about the person. As they are quite general, their validity is not questioned. On the other hand, this criticism does not stand up to critical and insightful astrological analyses that can reveal with great precision the personality traits of a client. We must remember also that most individuals do not have any very striking features, i.e., they occupy a position close to average regarding the personality. This means that they are neither properly extravert nor introvert, neither selfless nor selfish, disciplined or undisciplined, self-confident or insecure, liberal or conservative, but oscillate around the midpoint of the axis that counterpoints the two extremes.

Astrology is stagnant. It does not progress, it does not follow the development of science. Does this not mean that it will become increasingly distanced from the contemporary world and is about to become just a historical curiosity? This statement is almost true. The difficulty in understanding and validating the astrological phenomenon motivated its expulsion from the academic world. Regarded as mere superstition, astrology has suffered and continues to suffer severe setbacks. The rejection eventually consolidated a more intimate involvement with mysticism and the occult, resulting in it becoming out of step with the ways of contemporary science. It continued to keep a hard core of effective techniques that preserved the interest in astrology for centuries. Unfortunately, for giving up critical vision and almost completely disregarding the scientific method then emerging, it clung to dogma and "truths" that have become unquestionable. Mixed with the valid techniques are others, some totally useless, others not that reliable. It is for astrologers today to separate the wheat from the chaff.

Astrologers often say that the scientific method is not suitable to evaluate astrology. However, the scientific method has been used with great success to explain natural phenomena. Why should it be different with astrology? Is the supposed influence of the stars not part of the natural world? Many astrologers used to respond by saying that it is a phenomenon that is not part of the materialistic scientific view. It is, however, a comfortable stance and a regression to a pre-scientific past, which attributed supernatural causes to natural phenomena. The scientific method, yes, is suitable for assessing astrology, especially its results, when applied with proper understanding of how astrology really works. But it turns out it has been misused or misdirected, often deliberately, giving unfavorable results to astrology.

How can the old problem of the twins be solved? Whether they are identical or fraternal, having been born in the same place, the same day and about the same time, their charts should be the same, and their destinies should be the same too. But they are not. As the astrological chart does not predict destiny, there is no incompatibility between the existence of twins and astrology. This is a false problem.

The Pseudo-Skeptic War on Astrology

Astrology gets a lot of criticism from people in the academic world. Some of them reasoned and intelligent, some less so. Unfortunately, it is very common for the critic not to have the slightest notion of what astrology is, its history and the current state of this knowledge system. With simplistic approaches, often confusing astrology with Sun-sign columns, these scientists have done an unfortunate disservice to science and the "rationality" they defend.

In the twentieth century, the first large organized attack on astrology appeared in *The Humanist* magazine, conceived by philosophy professor and scientificist ideologist Paul Kurtz, editor of this publication. The diatribe took the form of a manifesto entitled "Objections to Astrology," signed by Bart J. Bok (astronomer), Lawrence E. Jerome (science journalist) and Paul Kurtz (professor of philosophy), and published in its September 1975 issue. Besides rehashing old arguments against astrology, discussing the danger posed by this type of "superstition" and "irrationalism" and calling astrologers charlatans, the only novelty was the addition of the signatures of 186 leading scientists, including 18 Nobel Award winners. It is interesting that none of these scientists had ever conducted any study of astrology nor presented a single piece of evidence to show this knowledge system to be false.

Not only astrologers have criticized the weakness of the "arguments" in the manifesto. Figures such as the psychologist Hans Eysenck, astronomer Carl Sagan and philosopher Paul Feyerabend repudiated its authoritarianism and lack of foundation. At the time, the astrological magazine *Aquarian Agent* received 187 signatures of people from the academic world contrary to the content of the manifesto (Eysenck & Nias, 1984).

Shortly after the episode of the manifesto, the controversy with the Gauquelin couple began. Not all members of the then created CSICOP (The Committee for the Scientific Investigation of Claims of the Paranormal) agreed with the methods used by Kurtz in conducting the experiment. Disgusted with the pranks of this astute professor of philosophy, Dennis Rawlins, skeptic, astronomer and member of CSICOP, wrote a devastating article for *Fate* magazine which denounced and exposed the entire set up behind the alleged verification of Gauquelin's Mars Effect. The episode became known as the sTARBABY Case, a story which incidentally is never told by pseudo-skeptics when they write their pretentious articles full of irony about Gauquelin, the Mars Effect, and astrology. Perhaps they overlook it due to embarrassment; perhaps they have not heard of it.

The sTARBABY Case

The fierce controversy surrounding the Gauquelin results and the Mars Effect prompted Marvin Zelen, a biostatistician and CSICOP member, to suggest a definitive test: check a new control group to see if the distribution of Mars for the average population would actually be seventeen percent in those two sectors. If approaching twenty-two percent, the value found by Gauquelin, this would invalidate the Mars Effect. According to Zelen, "Now we have an objective method to corroborate or refute. . . ."

One of the members of the Council, however, proved to be very worried. It was astronomer Dennis Rawlins, who later wrote the sTARBABY article for *Fate* magazine, denouncing the sham that the entire case involving the verification of the Mars Effect had become. Rawlins did not agree with the arguments that were being presented as he had already found some errors and foreseen problems because it appeared that at least Gauquelin's calculations were correct. Although also a skeptic, he saw no way to prove otherwise. If that was the case, why risk the reputation of CSICOP?

Almost a year later, according to the Rawlins' report, Gauquelin's original calculations had not yet been tested by Abell. Referring to the difficulty, Rawlins wrote: "His analysis . . . was based on an almanac provided by the U.S. Naval Observatory, which presented a list of the celestial longitudes of Mars in a fixed interval. Instead of using spherical trigonometry to convert the positions of Mars into equatorial coordinates (as demanded by the Gauquelin experiment), Abell persisted with the ecliptical coordinates of the Observatory program." At that time, Marcello Truzzi, then editor of *Skeptical Inquirer*, also began to disagree with articles that insisted on demographic explanations for the Mars Effect. Rawlins had even drafted mathematical explanations showing the errors of his skeptic colleagues.

The experiment, therefore, basically consisted of forming a new control group, grouping ordinary people born at the same time, from the same region of the champion athletes. First, Zelen wanted to use only 100 or 200 cases of the original sample of champions, from which the control group would be located. But this subsample was too small to detect the effect in question. Of course Gauquelin provided evidence of incorrect mathematical statistics that would result from this procedure. As a matter of practical viability, it was agreed that a subgroup of 303 champions would be sufficient. This sample resulted in 16,756 non-athletes as the control group. Zelen undertook a rigorous review of data and found the following values: 16.4 percent for the control group and 21.8 percent for the 303 champion athletes, as shown by Gauquelin's estimates. Subject closed? Not a chance.

In an article published by *Zetetic Scholar* in December 1982, Richard Kammann, professor of psychology at the University of Otago, New Zealand, wrote: "There is no doubt as to the undoubted victory of the Gauquelins in relation to the Mars Effect. Among 16,756 ordinary people, Mars was in sections one and four in 16.4 percent of their births, as expected, while for 2,088 European champions sportsmen, Mars occupied these sections in 21.6 percent of births, a difference entirely outside the realm of mere chance."

So what did the trio of pseudo-skeptics do? They divided the sample of 303 champions, which was already a subsample, into five subgroups, according to the specific region of origin and sources of data. In this manner, only one subgroup received a statistically significant result; the rest did not reach the minimum. Dramatically reducing the sample size, the Mars Effect disappeared. Michel Gauquelin himself, six months before, had already demonstrated that this would eliminate the planetary effect.

The pseudo-skeptics acted as if they were not aware of what was going on and started pointing out "disparities" and "anomalies" in the experiment. Not satisfied with the juggling they did, they removed the female champions from one of the sub-subsamples and women from the control group, making the result even less significant. The procedure itself was a true statistical aberration, an insult to science! Rawlins' warnings were of no avail, he himself an expert in planetary motion, and neither were the alerts from Elizabeth Scott, professor of statistics at the University of California-Berkeley, who was concerned about the consequences for the reputation of CSICOP.

The main report on the background of these incidents and their consequences was presented by Dennis Rawlings in an article he wrote for the October 1981 issue of *Fate* magazine, a publication specializing in the paranormal, new age, and similar subjects. The text is a ferocious attack aimed at former colleagues of CSICOP, denouncing the practice of some of these men, especially Paul Kurtz, in addressing the issue involving the Mars Effect nuisance. Rawlings then had been ousted from CSICOP.

Tarbaby is the name of the doll in a children's story by J. C. Harris. Every time the main character, Brer Rabbit, hit the doll, he became more stuck in the tar. This is the very same situation of the CSICOP trio: the more they sought to destroy Gauquelin's theory, the more they were entangled in their own mistakes and blunders, unable to get rid of that awful stellar viscosity.

Everything would become even worse when Kurtz, Abell and Zellen, tangled up with the European sample, decided to perform an independent test with sports champions born in the United States. This was trumpeted as a new "scientific" adventure in the November-December issue of *The Humanist*. They hammered out the details with Gauquelin during a meeting in July 1977. The skeptics would know what to do and how to conduct the experiment according to parameters accepted by both sides.

The data for the new test would be collected by CSICOP. Dissatisfied, however, with Abell, who took his time in taking action, Kurtz asked Rawlins to help and told him that this time he wanted to take a look at the results beforehand, to see what would happen. Kurtz sent the data and Rawlins calculated the positions of Mars. After the calculation of 120 names of athletes, sectors one and four amounted to twenty-two percent of the sample. Kurtz called Rawlins to learn the progress of the data and heard the bad news. Rawlins wrote:

> He groaned. I emphasized that the sample size was too small for the result to be statistically meaningful. He drew no comfort from this. I asked if he was sure that this was a clean sample. He said yes, so I assured him that the score was bound to revert to 17% as the sample got larger . . . unless astrological claims were true, which I certainly didn't believe. Nonetheless, he continued speaking in a pained voice, as someone cursed with a demon that would not go away.

On June 8, 1978, Rawlins concluded his work and sent a report to Kurtz with the results of 325 athletes. Shortly thereafter, Mr. Kurtz phoned to say: "Oops, we accidentally missed a lot of names . . . they'll be sent right away to the states' birth-record and we'll get the birth data back later this summer." At the end of summer there arrived another 82 names, totaling 407. With these latest figures, the final result was not twenty-two percent, nor seventeen percent, but, interestingly, thirteen and a half percent for the critical sectors one and four, thus discrediting the Mars Effect. Abell himself thought that the calculations were wrong or that the sample had been tampered with. Rawlins replied: "The sample came from Kurtz."

We cannot forget that Rawlins was also a skeptic, and therefore interested in a negative result for Gauquelin and astrology. Even though he revolted against the manipulations of his colleagues, in sTARBABY he did not openly question the final subsample of 82 names, which ends up producing a negative Mars Effect, well below the expected seventeen percent and dramatically below the twenty-two percent that had been occurring until then. But he also did not endorse it with enthusiasm.

The additions were made without Gauquelin's knowledge, who clearly suspected fraud. But Kurtz ignored his complaints. In fact, Kurtz had not fulfilled the main criteria arranged with Gauquelin: the athletes' excellence level and the inclusion in the sample of only individuals born through natural childbirth.

In 1983, Abell, Kurtz and Zelen published an article in *Skeptical Inquirer* in which they reassessed this episode in a posture of apparent retraction. They recognize that they were careless in their statements about the effectiveness of the Zelen test and that it was not possible to definitely resolve the question. That is, at the time they used the notorious pseudo-skeptic tactic of establishing criteria which, once achieved by the other party, are reconsidered and moved to higher levels of demand *ad eternum*. As they were defeated by Gauquelin, they justify by saying that the match did not count.

CSICOP

It was during the annual meeting of the American Humanist Association (AHA) in May 1976 that CSICOP, was founded. In addition to Paul Kurtz, chairman, Marcello Truzzi, Martin Gardner, James Randi and Ray Hyman joined the Committee as militant skeptics. The most moderate and balanced was Truzzi, who left the following year, disagreeing with the aggressiveness and radicalism of the other members. In the same year, CSICOP's magazine, *Skeptical Inquirer,* was born; its first editor was Kendrick Frazer. Below is what Lee Nisbet, executive director of CSICOP, said to *Science* magazine (Wade, 1977) on belief in the paranormal.

> . . . a very dangerous phenomenon, dangerous to science, dangerous to the basic fabric of our society . . . We feel it is the duty of the scientific community to show that these beliefs are utterly screwball . . .

The 1970s saw a growing interest in magic, Eastern philosophies, occultism, UFOs, parapsychology and astrology, and issues considered exotic by contemporary western culture and heresy by the fundamentalists of scientificism. The creation of CSICOP was a vigorous reaction to this cultural situation. One of the most criticized aspects in the orientation that the founders set for CSICOP was the form taken by their attacks on the pages of *Skeptical Inquirer*. Unlike the sober and objective tone found in texts written by scientists, *Skeptical Inquirer* accusations were aggressive, offensive articles, cartoons and caricatures that sought to expose their victims to ridicule. Everything that had to do with the so-called paranormal phenomena was ridiculed. Paranormals, seers and psychics were called quacks. The public was urged to unmask them. There was a large male predominance in CSICOP, which partly explains the intolerance, arrogance and verbal aggressiveness of its members. The researcher and parapsychologist George Hansen (1992), in his enlightening article on CSICOP, quotes the complaint of one of the few female skeptics attracted by this organization:

> I think another aspect of organized skepticism that may deter women is the aggressive, "macho" attitudes held by some of the (male) participants. It seems to me that some "skeptics" are more interested in ridicule than in exploring and challenging pseudoscientific beliefs.

Another interesting fact pointed out by some critics of pseudo-skepticism (Hansen, 1992; Leiter, 2002 and 2004) is the past beliefs of most of those who affiliate with a skeptical organization like CSICOP. There are a great number of skeptics who were either created by strict religious parents or they themselves, when young, enthusiastically believed in UFOs, spiritualist ideas and other similar ideas, but then became disillusioned and turned viciously against their old beliefs, willing to fight them at all costs, with a "rationality" that is very close to obsessive irrationality.

Since its creation CSICOP's strategy has been to reach as many people as possible. With his power of persuasion, Kurtz was able to attract into the ranks of the organization important names in science and philosophy, such as B. F. Skinner, Stephen Jay Gould, Francis Crick, Murray Gell-Mann, Carl Sagan, Karl Popper, W. V. Quine and Mario Bunge. The intellectual authority of these scientists and thinkers gave credibility to CSICOP because who would not be impressed with a team of this quality? However, it was not they who established the infamous policy of the Committee; they were not in power in the organization, making decisions and setting directions. This role was assumed mainly by Kurtz, professor of philosophy at the State University of New York- Buffalo; Martin Gardner, author and popularizer of the pseudo-skeptic ideology, trained in philosophy; and stage magician and showman James Randi, who ran away from school at age seventeen. They mocked and still mock parapsychologists who conduct high level research, and homeopathic physicians and acupunturists who develop major studies in their specialty, to name a few.

Unfortunately, CSICOP could exert a strong influence on the academic environment, especially influencing and forming opinions about parapsychology and the paranormal. Its avowed goal was to prevent research in this area and close laboratories that dared research parapsychology and related studies. Almost all of the scientists are unaware of the research conducted by parapsychologists and other scholars whose objective is to study anomalous or paranormal phenomena. Thus they accept the ideological terrorism perpetrated by CSICOP and other pseudo-skeptic organizations as scientific assessment and begin to call pseudo-science that which in truth they do not really know.

But the pinnacle of intolerance reached by this organization was the campaign to purchase shares of major television networks in order to have access to shareholder meetings so it could attempt to control the broadcast schedule by preventing shows from being presented. With this objective the Media Stock Fund was set up in 1997. To accomplish the ambitious goal, members were asked to donate money. CSICOP had a special tactic to get contributions from pseudo-skeptics anxious to teach the truth to those who still believed in superstitions. Following is an excerpt from a letter signed by a certain Barry Karr, director of CSICOP's Executive Council, requesting a contribution in cash or via credit card. After telling an unlikely story of a little girl who wrote to CSICOP claiming to be an alien, he blamed TV shows for promoting belief in paranormal phenomena.

> . . . Imagine if CSICOP never existed! Scary but true: CSICOP may be one of the last bulwarks against a future where children will grow up believing that they're aliens . . . or that folks wielding forked sticks can find water underground. To keep up the battle for rationality, I must ask you to make your most generous gift to CSICOP today.

In January 2007, CSICOP changed its name to Committee for Skeptical Inquiry or CSI, with headquarters in Amherst, New York, worth $4 million, and a center in Los Angeles valued at $5 million. Paul Kurtz is still head of the organization, and also chairman of the Council for Secular Humanism and publisher of Prometheus Books. The CSI headquarters is also the headquarters of the Commission for Scientific Medicine and Mental Health, which aims to combat alternative medicine.

Among the pseudo-skeptics, the most aggressive is James Randi, a magician. This man has no scientific training or qualifications, but asserts his right to criticize and slander serious researchers who develop studies in parapsychology and other non-orthodox knowledge systems, including astrology. His best known book is *Flim-Flam! Psychics, ESP, Unicorns and Other Delusions*. Writer Michael Prescott tells how Randi twists and invents facts in the book, and offends high-level researchers without presenting any evidence to support his generally categorical statements.

Astrology as a Pseudoscience

In her interesting masters' dissertation, Cristina de Amorim Machado (2006) addresses the problem of demarcation in the philosophy of science; that is, the separation between what is and what is not science, and the role of astrology as an example of pseudoscience according to the most diverse criteria. She cites five authors who mention astrology in their studies on the issue of demarcation: Karl Popper, Thomas Kuhn, Paul Feyerabend, Paul Thagard and Larry Laudan. Let's see what each of them has said, and if, indeed, astrology fits into their concept of pseudoscience.

A major concern of Popper and one of the most important points in his philosophy was the issue of demarcation between science and pseudoscience (or metaphysics). The criterion he developed was that of refutability or falsification, according to which a theory or a system of statements will only be truly scientific if it has a testable empirical content and, therefore, liable to be refuted or falsified. While acknowledging that astrology has "a large volume of empirical evidence based on observation," for him astrologers ignore evidence that contradicts their beliefs. Moreover, he said that astrological interpretations and "prophecies" are so vague that they can explain any refutation, which makes them not testable (Popper, K., 2002).

Now, if to some extent the criticism of Popper is not indeed without foundation, his own reference to astrology could not be more vague. What is this evidence? He never mentions these so-called interpretations and "prophecies." The references to astrology do not have any consistency. Popper touches a nerve of astrological theory, it is true, but he has no basis to support his assertion, as if that were unnecessary, self-evident, or a waste of time. Much more likely, however, is that Popper was unaware of the history of astrology and of how astrology works. In this he would not be very different from his peers. But ultimately, what exactly is being vague?

To understand this question, we must first define the nature of astrological prediction. Astrological analysis has to do with semantic domains or fields of meaning. From a psychological viewpoint it deals with personality traits and the dynamics of behavioral categories. Therefore, the astrology of our time does not anticipate events as such, nor what will happen with a person. What can be predicted are trends in behavior, both individually and in the social sphere, by extrapolation. There are no prophecies, as Popper erroneously imagines. There were, but in the past. But what astrology is he talking about? Is the astrology of antiquity the same as that of the Middle Ages? Both are indistinguishable from the contemporary? It is Popper who refers to astrology in such a vague way.

Kuhn (1979) notes that over the centuries many astrological predictions have failed. But it is certainly because they were not vague. Given their complexity, however, these failures, according to Kuhn, do not differ much from the mistakes made by medicine or meteorology or other sciences. So he rejects Popper's criterion, which does not separate established science from astrology. Yet for the author of *The Structure of Scientific Revolutions*, astrology is not a science but a technique that he compares to the medicine of past and contemporary psychoanalysis. It has rules to apply, but no riddle or puzzle to solve, and therefore no science to practice. Unlike astronomers, who, when faced with wrong forecast sought to correct the situation by checking data and observations, making new measurements, adjusting the theory, thus creating real puzzles, for Kuhn astrologers did not question the error, though they acknowledge the flaws. Thus the failures did not lead to what characterizes normal science, i.e., the solving of puzzles while articulating the paradigm.

Kuhn's interpretation requires more thorough historical research. The only reference he uses is the extensive treatise by Lynn Thorndyke, *A History of Magic and Experimental Science*, which obviously is not enough. In any case, the astrology that is practiced today is far from that which Kuhn and other critics superficially examine and hastily condemn. On the other hand, the attachment to the past unfortunately legitimates part of this critique, and a good part of the contents of my book is directed precisely at these deficiencies and seeks to heal them.

Paul R. Thagard wrote in 1978 an article entitled "Why Astrology is a Pseudoscience." Like Feyerabend, he cites some of Gauquelin's work, while Popper, Kuhn and Laudan do not seem to have heard of him. Early in the article Thagard says that "it would be most unfair to evaluate astrology by reference to the daily horoscopes found in newspapers and popular magazines." Wise words. He then criticizes the arguments of Bok, Lawrence and Kurtz that disqualify astrology based on its origin in magic. Thagard mentions chemistry and medicine, sciences whose roots date back to belief in magic and the occult. As for the possibility of a test, the statistical studies of Gauquelin are presented as examples of testability. Thagard briefly discusses its results without being biased. After questioning Popper's principle of falsifiability, he concludes that the falsification occurs only when there is actually a better theory.

But Thagard is a demarcationist and he ends up proposing a criterion, according to which a theory or discipline is pseudoscientific, if and only if: 1) It has been less progressive than alternative theories over a long period of time, and faces many unsolved problems; but 2) the community of practitioners makes little attempt to develop the theory towards solutions of the problems, shows no concern for attempts to evaluate the theory in relation to others, and is selective in considering confirmations and disconfirmations. (Thagard, P., 1998)

His claim that astrology is extremely non-progressive and has barely changed since Ptolemy seems exaggerated. After all, what does he mean by "barely changed"? Without presenting a historical overview, brief as it could be, of the development of astrological theory and its techniques, "barely changed" means little or nothing. It is a vague and unfounded assertion. So Thagard begins to compare astrology with other theories of personality and behavior that are more successful. Psychology, with its various branches, has developed much, much more than astrology. It is more reliable and is fully consolidated as a science; therefore it is a more progressive alternative.

Although astrology is not limited to a "theory of personality and behavior," the explanations which it presents are still confused and immature. But the perspective that it occupies allows you to introduce factors that need not necessarily compete with the relations of cause and effect studied by psychology; or better yet, are not opposed to them, even in a more naturalistic approach, as is the case in this book, which leaves aside ideas of non-causality, such as Jungian synchronicity. This is what we saw in the previous chapter, where I proposed a logic that relates, through the chemistry and physiology of the central nervous system, the cosmosphere of the solar system with human behavior and its personality traits.

Feyerabend, in his turn, in *The Strange Case of Astrology*, cast harsh criticism on the manifesto against astrology published by *The Humanist*. He denounced the authoritarian way the arguments were presented, as well as the ignorance of the subject by the scientists who put their names to it. "They certainly do not know what they are talking about," he noted. His methodological anarchism does not allow astrology to be discarded *a priori*, as do many scientists, and others (journalists, physicians, lawyers, etc.) who just repeat what the former state. That does not mean, however, that Feyerabend is an advocate of modern astrology, which, although it has inherited "interesting and profound ideas," for him it is a caricature of the past, now stagnated with its "naive rules."

Finally, Laudan shows that there never was a consensual understanding or definition for the scientific criterion most used from the nineteenth century: the scientific method. Still, being "scientific" or "unscientific" or even "pseudoscientific" necessarily brings social, political and economic implications. But, he states, as the demarcationist criteria failed to take into account the empirical scrutiny, "exotic" beliefs like astrology are to satisfy these criteria and could thus ensure the status of science. In any case, Laudan rejects the dichotomy between science and pseudoscience and prefers to think in terms of conceptual and empirical validity for knowledge.

Repentant Magdalenes

Astrology & Science (http://rudolfhsmit.nl/index) could be a good Web site to clarify the relationship between astrology and science. But there is a strong anti-astrology bias in almost all of the articles even though the authors affirm their impartiality and scientific spirit, whatever that means to them. The site is the work of Dutchman Rudolph Smit and counts on the participation of Geoffrey Dean, Arthur Mather and Ivan Kelly, former astrologers who have been engaged in a systematic campaign against astrology. Kelly is a psychologist. On their path they encountered CSICOP and banded together. In 1983, Dean was elected a member of CSICOP for "significant contributions to science and skepticism." Kelly is part of the subcommittee on astrology. Dean and Mather were the authors of *Recent Advances in Natal Astrology* published by the Astrological Association of England. It had a good reception despite controversy and the fact that some astrologers felt offended.

Articles written by Geoffrey Dean predominate. Some of these texts are signed by more than one writer, and there are also articles by other experts. But the message is almost always the same: astrology is an illusion and astrologers are naive and ignorant. Nevertheless, there is much useful information that can be drawn from here and there as long as the reader has the necessary critical thinking and separates the wheat from the chaff. But what motivates and encourages this crusade of former astrologers?

They were all astrologers once, wrote texts on astrology, attended conferences, stood out among their peers, but eventually persuaded themselves that astrology is an illusion, its allegations are false and astrologers are naive. They say they felt greatly deceived. Regretting their past, they decided to tell their story to the world, about their misguided experience and the "truth" they have now discovered.

Of the three repentant Magdalenes–Smit, Mather and Dean–the latter has been the most active. Dean's large number of articles that attempt to prove that astrology does not work is nothing but a silly waste of time. Each text is a new assault, always the same thing, always the same litany. Dean was a founder and first president of the western section (WA) of the Federation of Australian Astrologers, has a PhD in chemistry and worked in NATO. His book was an important milestone, no doubt. One might even say it was a milestone in the recent history of astrology due to the material collected and by the various issues raised. Perhaps that made Dean feel he held the power of life or death over astrology, one that could decide the fate of an entire ancient tradition. But ultimately, what made Dean, and also Mather and Smit, turn so furiously against this same astrology that once he even taught?

It seems that everything started with the book project. In the book, many criticisms are made of various aspects of practice and theory of astrology: an excessive amount of unreliable techniques, lack of method and objectivity in interpretation, symbols with vague meanings, unsubstantiated beliefs, hypotheses taken as truth, presuppositions rather than proof, texts that lack clarity and organization, and the lack of worry about validation of astrological knowledge. Despite many negative points, Dean and Mather concluded: "The emerging picture suggests that astrology works, but hardly in the manner or extent which it is presented." Unfortunately, in general, the comments by Dean and Mather on the astrological praxis are not entirely incorrect. Later, however, they radicalized their position and ruled out any validity for the astrological phenomenon. More than that, they started, in the company of CSICOP, orchestrating a systematic campaign against astrology, a crusade, with support from pseudo-skeptic organizations.

Dean, Mather and Smit could simply have walked away from the astrological community and continued their lives in another direction. From the moment they no longer believed in astrology, it is understandable that they wanted to express this apostasy through critical texts. So far, that is nothing unusual. But what stands out is the intensity and constancy of the attacks. The trio of former astrologers took up the same stance as Paul Kurtz and his men. However, he remained involved with astrological organizations under the guise of an impartial researcher seeking the truth. As a consultant for *Correlation*, and working along the lines of scientific journals, Dean became a sort of pseudo-skeptical Trojan horse fighting behind enemy lines. The other astrologers who wrote for *Correlation* allowed Dean to control much of the space in the magazine. His articles were the longest, the most frequent and always sought to discredit astrology and astrologers. Mr. Kurtz must have been very pleased with his disciple.

In 1993, Rudolf Smit was named the new editor of *Correlation*, and stated in one of his articles entitled "Astrology: My Passion, My Life, My Personal Disaster" that due to disillusionment with astrology he fell into a depressive state that lasted for years and which ended up costing him a marriage. This happened in the mid-1980s. Why after such bitter disappointment would Smit accept the post of *Correlation* editor? Almost six years later, in December 1988, Pat Harris took over the editorship; she is an astrologer truly committed to her craft and not with militant scientificism. In 2002, Dean and Smit left *Correlation*.

One of the problems most emphasized, mainly by Dean and Smit, is the question of "the wrong chart." This happened with them and with other experts. The astrologer reads the chart and the client is very impressed with the precision his or her personality and some circumstances of his or her life are described. But then the astrologer realizes that he or she has used the wrong chart and was therefore interpreting the data of someone else's chart. Even so, according to the client, the description matched perfectly. Interpretations have also been made of historical figures with data that later turned out to be incorrect. These mistakes strengthen the argument that the client wanted to believe what was heard or that the reading was of a very general nature. In the case of adjusting the chart reading, whatever that is, to the characteristics of a public figure, this is possible because the astrologer blends the variables available with such freedom that he can easily describe, with great precision, personality traits, qualities and events that are widely known. Here, method, criteria, and a more refined technique are missing.

Chapter 7

Final Remarks

Despite the adversity and prejudice astrology has faced from among so-called "intellectuals," it is still alive and breathing, and we can say that it has grown, not as much as we wanted it to, but it has grown. It developed, yes, entirely at the margin of scientific orthodoxy, and from the 1960s returned to take part in the day-to-day life of Western culture, possibly as a mere curiosity to some, but for others as another vision of reality. Of course, its current absence from universities and other institutions that could finance and foster the study of this ancient system of knowledge is not good. Astrology has been drawn ever closer to the esoteric and mystical side of life. I have nothing against the occult, but this trend pushed astrology through paths not followed by science or by the traditional religions.

Organizations led by skeptics or pseudo-skeptics, have tried since the 1970s to attack astrology in many different ways. They ridicule astrologers, label us as charlatans, swindlers and impostors, and when they "praise" us, we are superstitious and enemies of reason. They constantly seek to boycott any inclusion of astrology in academic curricula, especially in research and studies using astrological techniques. Only those efforts to prove that astrology does not work are valid. This is a kind of ideological terrorism practiced by people who consider themselves of a superior intellect and who succeed in imposing their agenda of orthodox prejudice in universities. The message is: science alone knows the truth; the rest is ignorance and superstition. They almost always avoid criticizing religion because they fear its social and political power, but religions practiced by minorities are also violated. Fortunately, these crude materialists do not represent current scientific thinking, just part of it. I would say they do not even represent materialism, especially its smarter branches.

Nevertheless, astrology will keep on going, showing its remarkable resilience. Insisting on a more intimate connection between human beings, their planetary nest and the cosmosphere, it attracts the attention of sensitive people that in a way see its reality intuitively. It lacks, however, a dialogue with the present time, with the science that pervades and builds the world today. Gradually, however, there is an approach. Astrologers realize that the initiative should come from them, not to beg for acceptance, but to show their craft and conquer that social space so necessary to the development of any human knowledge. Furthermore, we have learned to avoid traps set by pseudo-skeptics in the form of "scientific experiments." Invariably a pseudo-skeptic organization would be happy to verify "with objectivity and impartiality" the claims of astrology. If the result was in their favor, they would be content; otherwise they would be ready with an argument on the tip of their tongues, and another and another, whenever they could not prove what they wanted to prove.

In this book I present my modest contribution to a contemporary astrology. The scientific method, when used in honest and relevant ways, no doubt is a powerful and indispensable tool to the development of astrological knowledge. But applying it and ignoring the how-to of the astrology practice is useless. Real astrology is the practical exercise of its principles and techniques. There is no point in criticizing it or trying to verify its true value when you do not know the universe of its practice. Cutting it into slices to see if the pieces are real is not always the best option. Disregard of the specificity of its language is another very common misconception. Comparisons should be made very carefully, knowing very well the two sides to be compared. Another important issue is the construction of more robust theoretical models. With this work, I try to lay some bricks and hope to continue this building project along with other fellow astrologers.

Bibliography

Abell, G., Kurtz, P., and Zelen, M. 1983. "The Abell-Kurtz-Zelen Mars Effect Experiments: A Reappraisal." *Skeptical Inquirer*, 7(3), 77-82.

Albuquerque, L. M. B. 2003. *Sujeito E Realidade Na Ciência Moderna*. São Paulo: Annablume.

Allport, G. W. 1966. *Personalidade: Padrões E Desenvolvimento*. São Paulo: Herder.

Archer, J. 2004. "Testosterone And Human Aggression: An Evaluation of the Challenge Hypothesis," *Neuroscience and Biobehavioral Reviews*, 30, 319-345.

Bains, P. 2001. Umwelten. *Semiotica*, 134, 137-167.

Bannerman, D. M. et al. 2004. "Regional Dissociations Within the Hippocampus—Memory and Anxiety." *Neuroscience and Biobehavioral Reviews*, 28, 273-283.

Barbault, A. *Un Siècle De Statistiques Astrologiques* (http://www.andrebarbault.com/siecle_stats.htm).

Barrett, L. F. and Wager, T. D. 2006. "The Structure of Emotion: Evidence from Neuroimaging Studies." *Current Directions in Psychological Science*, 15 (2), 79-83.

Bartz, J. A. and Hollander, E. 2006. "The Neuroscience of Affiliation: Forging Links Between Basic and Clinical Research on Neuropeptides and Social Behavior." *Hormones and Behavior*, 50, 518-528.

Bell, C. J. et al. 2006. "Plasma Oxytocin Levels in Depression and Their Correlation with the Temperament Dimension of Reward Dependence." *Journal of Psychopharmacology*, 20 (5), 656-660.

Benjamin, J., Ebstein, R. P., and Lesch, K. 1998. "Genes for Personality Traits: Implications for Psychopathology." *International Journal of Neuropsychopharmacology*, 1, 153-168.

Benski, C. et al. 1996. *The Mars Effect*. Amherst: Prometheus Books.

Benveniste, E. 1989. *Problemas de Linguística Geral II*. Campinas: Pontes Editores.

Bok, B. J. and Jerome, L. E. 1975. *Objections to Astrology*. Buffalo: Prometheus Books.

Bond, A. J. 2001. "Neurotransmitters, Temperament And Social Functioning." *European Neuropsychopharmacology*, 11, 261-274.

Briggs, S. R. 1989. "The Optimal Level Of Measurement For Personality Constructs." In D.M. Buss, N. Cantor (eds.), *Personality Psychology: Recent Trends and Emerging Directions* (Chapter 18). New York: Springer-Verlag.

Buss, A. H. 1989. "Personality as Traits." *American Psychologist*, 44, 11, 1378-1388.

Canli, T. et al. (2001). "An fMRI Study of Personality Influences on Brain Reactivity to Emotional Stimuli." *Behavioral Neuroscience*, 115(1), 33-42.

Canli, T. 2004. "Functional Brain Mapping of Extraversion and Neuroticism: Learning from Individual Differences in Emotion Processing." *Journal of Personality*, 72(6), 1105-1132.

Carlson, S. 1985. *A Double-Blind Test Of Astrology*. Nature, 318 (5), 419-425.

Castille, D. 1999. *Sunny Day For A Wedding*, http://www.ramsfr.fr/castille02us.pdf.

Castille, D. 2002. *Questioning Methods*, http://cura.free.fr/xxv/21cas4en.html.

Chalmers, A. (1994) A Fabricação da ciência. São Paulo: Ed. UNESP.

Clarke, D., Gabriels, T. and Barnes, J. 1996. "Astrological Signs as Determinants of Extraversion and Emotionality: An Empirical Study." *The Journal of Psychology*, 130(2), 131-140.

Cloninger, C. R. 1987. "A Systematic Method For Clinical Description And Classification of Personality Variants." *Archives of General Psychiatry*, 44, 573-588.

Cohen, M.X. et al. 2005. "Individual Differences in Extraversion and Dopamine Genetics Predict Neural Reward Responses," *Cognitive Brain Research*, 25, 851-861.

Colapietro, V. 1991. "Two Rivals Conceptions of the Semiological Ideal: Peirce Versus Saussure." *Face*, 1: 135-158.

Cooper, G. M. 1999. *Galen's "On Critical Days": Greek Medicine in Arabic*. Doctoral thesis, Columbia University.

Cooter, R. 1982. The Conservatism of "Pseudoscience." (In Grim, Patrick (ed.): *Philosophy of Science and the Occult*. Albany: State University of New York Press.

Cory, G. A. 2002. "MacLean's Evolutionary Neuroscience, the CSN Model and Hamilton's Rule: Some Developmental, Clinical, and Social Policy Implications." *Brain and Mind*, 3, 151-181.

Crowe, R. A. 1990. "Astrology and the Scientific Method." *Psychological Reports*, 67, 163-191.

Culver, R. B. and Ianna, P. A. 1984. *The Gemini Syndrome: A Scientific Evaluation of Astrology*. Buffalo: Prometheus Books.

Dalgleish, T. 2004. "The Emotional Brain." *Nature Reviews, Neuroscience*, vol 5, 582-589.

Dahlstrom, W. G. et al. 1996. "MMPI findings on astrological and other folklore concepts of personality." *Psychological Reports*, 78, 1059-1070.

Davidson, R. J. and Irwin, W. 1999. "The Fonctional Neuroanatomy of Emotion and Affective Style," *Trends in Cognitive Sciences*, 3, (1), 11-21.

De Fruyt, F. et al. 2000. "Cloninger's Psychobiological Model of Temperament and Character and the Five-Factor Model of Personality." *Personality and Individual Differences*, 29, 441-452.

Dean, G. *The Gauquelin Work 1: a Concise History with Photographs*, http://www.rudolfhsmit.nl/g-hist2.htm.

Dean, G. 1977. *Recent Advances in Natal Astrology*. Western Australia: Analogical Press.

Deely, J. 1990. *Semiótica Básica*. São Paulo: Ática.

Deely, J. 2001. *Umwelt*. Semiotica, 134, 1/4, 125-135.

Discepolo, C. and Miele, L. *Osservazioni Politematiche Sulle Richerche Discepolo/Miele*, http://www.programmiastral.com/osservazioni.pdf.

Dubois, J. et al. 2001. *Dicionário de Linguística*. São Paulo: Cultrix.

Dunlop, B. W. and Nemeroff, C. B. 2007. "The Role of Dopamine in the Pathophysiology of Depression." *Archives of General Psychiatry*, 64, 327-337.

Ebstein, R. P. et al. 1996. "Dopamine D4 Receptor (D4DR) Exon III Polymorphism Associated with the Human Personality Trait of Novelty Seeking." *Nature Genetics*, 12, 78-80.

Edinger, E. F. 2000. *A Psique na Antiguidade*. São Paulo: Cultrix.

Epstein, I. 2002. *O Signo*. São Paulo: Ática.

Epstein, S. 1983. "Aggregation and Beyond: Some Basic Issues on the Prediction of Behavior." *Journal of Personality*, 51, 360-392.

Ertel. S. 1990. "Scrutinizing Gauquelin's Character Trait Hypothesis Once Again." *Correlation*, 10(2), 3-19.

Ertel, S. 1993. "Why the Character Trait Hypothesis Still Fails." *Correlation*, 12(1), 2-9.

Ertel, S. (n/d) "On Dr. Nienhuys' Stamping the Evidence for a Mars Effect Based on the CFEPP's Athletes Data."

Ertel, S. and Irving, K. (n/d) The Mars Effect in Prospect: Dissenting from J.W. Nienhuys' "Retrospect." (http://www.planetos.info/dissent.html)

Ertel, S. and Irving, K. (1996) *The Tenacious Mars Efffect*. Londres: The Urania Trust.

Ertel, S. and Irving, K. (2000) "The Mars Effect is Genuine: on Kurtz, Nienhuys, and Sandhu's Missing the Evidence." *Journal of Scientific Exploration*, 14, 421-430.

Eysenck, H. J. e Eysenck, M. W. (1985) *Personality and Individual Differences*. Nova York: Plenum.

Eysenck, H.J. e Nias, D.K.B. (1984) *Astrology: Science or Superstition?* Pelican Books.

Feyerabend, P.K. (1970) Consolando o Especialista. In Lakatos, I. and Musgrave, A. (org.): A crítica e o desenvolvimento do conhecimento. São Paulo: Cultrix/EDUSP.

Feyerabend, Paul K. (1982) "The Strange Case of Astrology" (In Grim, Patrick (ed.): *Philosophy of Science and the Occult*. Albany: State University of New York Press.)

Forer, B.R. (1949) "The Fallacy of Personal Validation: a Classroom Demonstration of Gullibility." *Journal of Abnormal and Social Psychology*, 44, 118-123.

Fourie, D.P. (1984) "Self-attribution Theory and the Sun-sign." *The Journal of Social Psychology*, 122, 121-126.

Fowles, D.C. (2006) Jeffrey Gray's contributions to theories of anxiety, personality, and psychopatology; in Canli, T. (ed.), *Biology of Personality and Individual Differences* (Chap 2). New York: The Guilford Press.

Fraknoi, A. (n/d) "Your Astrology Defense Kit." (http://www.astrosociety.org/education/astro/act3/astrology3.html#defense)

Friedman, H. S. e Schustack, M.W. (2004) *Teorias da Personalidade*. São Paulo: Prentice Hall.

Fuller, M. and Dobson, J. 2005. "On the Significance of the Time Constants of Magnetic Field Sensitivity in Animals," *Bioeletromagnetics*, 26, 234-237.

Fuzeau-Braesch, S. 1990. *A Astrologia*. São Paulo: Jorge Zahar.

Gallinat, J. et al. 2007. "Association Between Cerebral Glutamate and Human Behaviour: the Sensation Seeking Personality Trait," *NeuroImage*, 34, 671-678.

Gauquelin, F. 1995. "CTH Soon Acceptable to Professor Ertel?", *Correlation*, 14(2), 27-28.

Gauquelin, M. 1955. *L'Influence des Astres*. Paris: Du Dauphin.

Gauquelin, M. 1960. *Les Hommes et les Astres*. Paris: Éditions Denoël.

Gauquelin, M. 1970. *The Scientific Basis of Astrology*. New York: Stein and Day.

Gauquelin, M. 1973. *Rythmes Biologiques, Rythmes Cosmiques*. Verviers: Marabout.

Gauquelin, M. 1978. *A Cosmopsicologia*. Lisboa: Ática.

Gauquelin, M. 1979. *Dreams and Illusions of Astrology*. Londres: Glover & Blair Ltd.

Gauquelin, M. 1982. *Cosmic Clocks*. San Diego: Astro Computing Services.

Gauquelin, M. 1983) *Birthtimes: A Scientific Investigation of the Secrets of Astrology*. New York: Hill and Wang.

Gauquelin, M. 1985. *Cosmic Influences on Human Behavior*. New York: Aurora Press.

Gauquelin, M. 1988. *Planetary Heredity*. San Diego: ACS Publications.

Gauquelin, M. 1988. "Is there really a Mars Effect?", *Journal of Scientific Exploration*, 2(1), 29-51.

Gauquelin, M. 1991. *Neo-astrology: a Copernican Revolution*. Londres: Arkana.

Gauquelin. M., Gauquelin, F. and Eysenck. S. B. G. 1979. "Personality and Position of the Planets at Birth: An Empirical Study," *British Journal of Social and Clinical Psychology*, 18, 71-75.

Gauquelin. M., Gauquelin, F. and Eysenck. S.B.G. 1981. "Eysenck's Personality Analysis and Position of the Planets at Birth: A Replication on America Subjects," *Personality and Individual Differences*, 2, 346-350.

Gauquelin, M. and Tracz, S. 1990. "Gauquelin's Character Trait Hypothesis: the Fresno Experiment," *Correlation*, 10(2), 20-33.

Gazzaniga, M. S. and Heatherton, T. F. 2005. *Ciência Psicológica: Mente, Cérebro e Comportamento*. Porto Alegre: Artmed.

Glasnapp, D. R. and Poggio, J. P. 1985. *Essentials of Statistical Analysis for the Behavioral Sciences*. Columbus: Charles E. Merril.

Goldberg, L. R. 1993. "The Structure of Phenotypic Personality Traits." *American Psychologist*, 48, 1, 26-34.

Golimbet, V. E. et al. 2007. "Relationship Between Dopamine System Genes and Extraversion and Novelty Seeking." *Neuroscience and Behavioral Physiology*, 37 (6), 601-606.

Gordon, C. and Berk, M. 2003. "The Effect of Goemagnetic Storms on Suicide." *South African Psychiatry Review*, 6, 24-27.

Greene, L. and Sasportas, H. 1994. *Os Luminares*. São Paulo: Roca.

Greene, L. and Sasportas, H. 1995. *Os Planetas Interiores*. São Paulo: Roca.

Greimas, A. J. 1973. *Semântica Estrutural*. São Paulo: Cultrix.

Guttman, L. 1954. "A New Approach to Factor Analysis: the radex." In Lazarsfeld, P. F. (ed.) *Mathematical Thinking in the Social Sciences*. Glencoe: The Free Press.

Hall, C. S., Lindzey, G. and Campbell, J. B. 2000. *Teorias da Personalidade*. Porto Alegre: Artmed.

Hampson, S.E, Gilmour, R. and Harris, P. L. (1978) Accuracy in Self-perception: the Fallacy of Personal Validation." *British Journal of Social and Clinical Psychology*, 17, 231-235.

Hansen, G. P. 1992. "CSICOP and the Skeptics: An Overview." *The Journal of American Society for Psychical Research*, 88 (1), 19-63.

Harris, J. C. 2003. "Social Neuroscience, Empathy, Brain Integration, and Neurodevelopmental Disorders." *Physiology & Behavior*, 79, 525-531.

Hartmann, P., Reuter, M. and Nyborg, H. 2006. "The Relationship Between Date of Birth and

Individual Differences in Personality and General Intelligence: A Large-scale Study." *Personality and Individual Differences,* 40, 1349-1362.

Jackson, M. 1979. "Extraversion, Neuroticism and Date of Birth: A Southern Hemisphere Study." *The Journal of Psychology,* 101, 197-198.

Jackson, M. and Fiebert, M. S. 1980. "Introversion-extraversion and Astrology." *The Journal of Psychology,* 105, 155-156.

Jerome, L. E. 1975. "Astrology: Magic or Science." *The Humanist,* 35 (5), 10-16.

John, O. P. and Srivastava, S. 1999. "The Big-Five Trait Taxonomy: History, Measurement and Theoretical Perspectives." (In Pervin, L. and John, O. P. (eds.), *Handbook of Personality: Theory and Research,* 2nd ed., New York: Guilford).

Johnsen, S. and Lohmann, K. J. 2005. The Physics and Neurobiology of Magnetoreception. *Nature Reviews, Neuroscience,* 6, 703-712.

Jouanna, J. 1999. *Hippocrates.* Londres: The Johns Hopkins University Press.

Jung, C. G. 1987. *Tipos Psicológicos.* Rio de Janeiro: Guanabara Koogan.

Jung. C. G. 1988. *Memórias, Sonhos, Reflexões.* Rio de Janeiro: Nova Fronteira.

Jung. C. G. 1997. *Sincronicidade.* Petrópolis: Vozes.

Jung. C. G. 2000. *Os Arquétipos e o Inconsciente Coletivo.* Petrópolis: Vozes.

Jung. C. G. 2002. *Cartas de C. G. Jung (Vol I, 1906-1945).* Petrópolis:Vozes.

Jung. C. G. 2002. *Cartas de C. G. Jung (Vol II, 1946-1955).* Petrópolis:Vozes.

Jung. C. G. 2003. *Cartas de C. G. Jung (Vol III, 1956-1961).* Petrópolis:Vozes.

Kammann, R. 1982. "The True Disbelievers: Mars Effect Drives Skeptics to Irrationality." *Zetetic Scholar,* 10, 50-65.

Kant, I. 1993. *Anthropologie du Point de Vue Pragmatique.* Paris: Flammarion.

Kay, R. W. 1994. "Geomagnetic Storms: Association with Incidence of Depression as Measured by Hospital Admission." *British Journal of Psychiatry,* 164, 403-409.

Keightley, M. L. et al. 2003. "Personality Influences Limbic-cortical Interactions During Sad Mood Induction." *NeuroImage,* 20, 2031-2039.

Kelly, I. W. "Vested Interests 1, Scientific Integrity 0: the Decline and Fall of the AA's Journal *Correlation.*" http://www.rudolfhsmit.nl/d-vest2.htm.

Kelly, I. W. 1997. "Modern Astrology: A Critique." *Psychological Reports,* 81, 1035-1066.

Klibansky, R, Panofsky, E. and Saxl, F. 1989. *Saturne et la Mélancolie.* Paris: Gallimard.

Kuhn, T. S. 1970. *The Structure of Scientific Revolutions,* 2nd ed. Chicago: The University of Chicago Press.

Kuhn, T. S. 1979. "Lógica da Descoberta ou Psicologia da Pesquisa?" In Lakatos, I. and Musgrave, A. (org.): *A Crítica e o Desenvolvimento do Conhecimento*. São Paulo: Cultrix/EDUSP.)

Kull, K. 2001. "Jakob von Uexküll: An Introduction." *Semiotica*, 134, 1/4 1-59.

Kurtz, P. 1977. "The Psychology of Belief." *Humanist*, 37(3), 42-43.

LaForge, R. 1985. The Early Development of the Freedman-Leary-Coffey Interpersonal System. *Journal of Personality Assessment*, 49 (6), 623-621.

Lakatos, I. and Musgrave, A. 1979. *A Crítica e o Desenvolvimento do Conhecimento*. São Paulo: Cultrix/EDUSP.

Laudan, L. 1996. *Beyond Positivism and Relativism*. Boulder: Westview Press.

Leary, T. 2004. *Interpersonal Diagnosis of Personality*. Eugene: Resource Pub.

LeDoux, J. 1993. "Emotional Networks in the Brain. In Lewis, M. and Haviland, J. M. (eds.), *Handbook of Emotions* (Chapter 8). New York: The Guilford Press.

LeDoux, J. 2001. *O Cérebro Emocional*. Rio de Janeiro: Objetiva.

Legrand, G. 1991. *Os Pré-Socráticos*. São Paulo: Jorge Zahar.

Leiter, D. L. 2002 "The Pathology of Organized Skepticism." *Journal of Scientific Exploration*, 16, 1, 125-128.

Leiter, D. L. 2004. "Organized Skepticism Revisited." *Journal of Scientific Exploration*, 18, 4, 661-664.

Lent, R. 2001. *Cem bilhões de Neurônios: Conceitos Fundamentais de Neurociência*. São Paulo: Atheneu.

Lewin, K. 1973. *Princípios de Psicologia Topológica*. São Paulo: Cultrix.

Lohmann, K. J. and Johsen, S. 2000. "The Neurobiology of Magnetoreception in Vertebrate Animals." *Trends in Neuroscience*, 23, 153-159.

Longrigg, J. 1993. *Greek Rational Medicine: Philosophy and Medicine from Alcmeon to the Alexandrians*. Londres: Routledge.

Longrigg, J. 2001. *Greek Medicine: from the Heroic to the Hellenistic Age*. Londres: Duckworth.

Machado, C. A. 2006. "A Falência dos Modelos Normativos da Ciência–a Astrologia Como um Estudo de Caso." Master's thesis, PUC-Rio.

MacLean, P. 1983. "Brain Roots of the Will-to-Power." *Zygon*, 18, 4, 359-374.

MacLean, P. 1990. *The Triune Brain in Evolution*. Nova York: Plenum Press.

MacLean, P. 1993. "Cerebral Evolution of Emotion." In Lewis, M. and Haviland, J. M. (eds.),

Handbook of Emotions (Chapter 6). New York: The Guilford Press.

Manilius. *Astronomica*. Trans. by G. P. Goold, 1977.

March, M. D. and McEvers, J. 1996. *Curso Básico de Astrologia*, vols I e II. São Paulo: Pensamento.

Mayo, J., White, O. and Eysenck, H. J. 1978. "An Empirical Study of the Relation Between Astrological Factors and Personality." *The Journal of Social Psychology*, 105, 229-236.

McCrae, R. R. and Costa, P. T., Jr. 1997. "Personality Trait Structure as a Human Universal." *American Psychologist*, 52, 5, 509-516.

McCrae, R. R. and Costa, P. T., Jr. 2006. *Personality in Adulthood: a Five-Factor Theory Perspective*. New York: The Guilford Press.

McCrae, R. R. and John, O. P. 1992. "An Introduction to the Five-Factor Model and its Applications." *Journal of Personality*, 60, 175-215.

McGillion, F. 2002. "The Pineal Gland and the Ancient Art of Iatromathematica." *Journal of Scientific Exploration*, 16, 19-43.

McGrew, J. H. and McFall, R. M. 1992. "A Collaborative Vernon Clark Experiment." *Correlations*, 11(2), 2-10.

McLynn, F. 1998. *Carl Gustav Jung: Uma Biografia*. Rio de Janeiro: Record.

Micek, S. and Micek, G. 2005. "Are the Earth Magnetic Field and Schumann Resonance Related to Global Human Activity?" *Bio-Algorithms and Med-Systems*, 1, 301-306.

Mobbs, D. et al. 2005. "Personality Predicts Activity in Reward and Emotional Regions Associated with Humor." Proceedings of the National Academy of Sciences of the USA, 102 (45), 16502-16506.

Morgane, P. J. et al. 2005. "A Review of Systems and Networks of the Limbic Forebrain/limbic Midbrain." *Progress in Neurobiology*, 75, 143-160.

Morin, J. B. (1661) *Astrologia Gallica Book Twenty One*. Trans. to the English by Richard S. Baldwin (1974), Washington: American Federation of Astrologers.

Mourão, R. R. F. 1995. Dicionário Enciclopédico de Astronomia e Astronáutica. Rio de Janeiro: Nova Fronteira.

Mueller, F. L. 1968. *História da Psicologia*. São Paulo: Cia Editora Nacional.

Muheim, R. 2001. "Animal Magnetoreception: Models, Physiology and Behaviour." Introductory Paper nº 128, Dept of Ecology, Lund University.

Nanninga, R. 1996/97. "The Astrotest: A Tough Match for Astrologers." *Correlations*, 15(2), 14-20.

Noblett, K.L. and Coccaro, E.F. 2005. "Molecular Genetics of Personality." *Current Psychiatry*

Reports, 7, 73-80.

Noll, R. .1996. *O Culto de Jung: Origens de um Movimento Carismático*. São Paulo: Ática.

Noll, R. 1997. *The Aryan Christ: The Secret Life of Carl Jung*. New York: Random House.

Northcutt, R. G. and Kaas, J. H. 1995. "The Emergence and Evolution of Mammalian Neocortex." *Trends in Neuroscience*, 18, 9, 373-379.

Nöth, W. 1998. *Ecosemiotics*. Sign Systems Studies, 26, 332-343.

Panchelyuga, V. A. and Shnoll, S. E. "Experimental Investigation of Spinning Massive Body Influence on Fine Structure of Distribution Functions of α-decay Rate Fluctuations." http://arxiv.org/ftp/physics/papers/0606/0606173.pdf

Panksepp, J. 1993. "Neurochemical Control of Moods and Emotions: Amino Acids to Neuropeptides." (Em Lewis, M. and Haviland, J. M. (eds.), *Handbook of Emotions* (Chapter 7). New York: The Guilford Press.

Paris, J. 2005. "Neurobiological Dimensional Models of Personality: A Review of the Models of Cloninger, Depue, and Sever." *Journal of Personality Disorders*, 19(2), 156-170.

Parker, J. and Parker, D. 2003. *Parker's Astrology*. Londres: Dorling Kindresley.

Peirson, A. R. et al. 1999. "Relationship Between Serotonin and the Temperament and Character Inventory." *Psychiatry Research*, 89, 29-37.

Peirce, C. S. 1972. *Semiótica e Filosofia: Textos Escolhidos de Charles Sanders Peirce*. São Paulo: Cultrix.

Pellegrini, R. J. 1973. "The Astrological "Theory" of Personality: An Unbiased Test by a Biased Observer." *The Journal of Psychology*, 1973, 85, 21-28.

Pervin, L. A. and John, O. P. 2004. *Personalidade: Teoria e Pesquisa*. Porto Alegre: Artmed.

Peters, R. S. 1953. *Brett's History of Psychology*. Londres: George Allen & Unwin.

Phillipson, G. .2000. *Astrology in the Year Zero*. Londres: Flare Publications.

Pinch, T. J. and Collins, H. M. 1984. "Science and Public Knowledge: The Committee for the Scientific Investigation of the Claims of the Paranormal and its Use of the Literature." *Social Studies of Science*, 14(4), 521-546.

Pinel, J.P.J. (2005) Biopsicologia. Porto Alegre: Artmed.

Popper, K. (1985) A lógica da pesquisa científica. São Paulo: Cultrix.

Popper, K. (2002) Conjectures and refutations. Nova York: Routledge.

Prescott, M. "A Skeptical Look at James Randi." http://www.skepticalinvestigations.org/exam/Prescott_Randi.

Ptolemy, C. *Tetrabiblos*. Trans. by F. E. Robbins, 1948.

Raitzin, C. Jean Baptiste Morin de Villefranche. "Una Sintesis de Su Vida y de Su Obra Astrologica." http://www.spicasc.net/villefra.htm.

Randi, J. 1980. *Flim-Flam! Psychics, ESP, Unicorns, and Other Delusions.* Amherst: Prometheus Books.

Rang, H. P., Dale, M. M. and Ritter, J. M. 2001. *Farmacologia,* 4th ed. Rio de Janeiro: Guanabara Koogan.

Rawlins, D. 1981. "sTARBABY." *Fate,* 34, 67-98. http://cura.free.fr/xv/14starbb.html.

Reale, G. and Antiseri, D. 2006. *História da Filosofia,* vol 7. São Paulo: Paulus.

Roberts, P. and Greengrass, H. 1994. *The Astrology of Time Twins.* Auckland: Pentland Press.

Rochberg-Halton, F. 1988. "Elements of the Babylonian contribuiton to Hellenistic Astrology." *Journal of the American Oriental Society,* vol. 108, 1, 51-62.

Rochberg, F. 1999. "Empiricism in Babylonian Omen Texts and the Classification of Mesopotamian Divination as Science." *Journal of the American Oriental Society,* 119 (4), 559-569.

Rodrigues, P. R. G. 1997. "Astrologia, Meio Ambiente e Personalidade: um Estudo Empírico." Master's thesis, Instituto de Psicologia, USP.

Ronan, Colin A. 1987. *História Ilustrada da Ciência,* Vol 1, p. 97-99. São Paulo: Jorge Zahar.

Rooij, J. van, Brak, M. A. and Commandeur, J. F. 1988. "Introversion-Extraversion and Sun-sign." *The Journal of Psychology,* 122(3), 275-278.

Russel, J. and Wagstaff, G. F. 1983. "Extraversion, Neuroticism and Time of Birth." *British Journal of Social Psychology,* 22, 27-31.

Saklofske, D. H., Kelly, I. W. and McKerracher, D. W. 1982. "An Empirical Study of Personality and Astrological Factors." *The Journal of Psychology,* 110, 275-280.

Santaella, L. 2000. *A Teoria Geral Dos Signos.* São Paulo: Pioneira.

Santoni, F. 2002. "A century of Scientific Astrology in France." http://www.uranian-institute.org/fscentsci.htm.

Scheifler, D. S. S. "Recado Astrológico: O Baile de João Guimarães Rosa." http://www.mafua.ufsc.br/danielasevero.html.

Schultheiss-Grassi, P. P., Wessiken, R. and Dobson, J. 1999. "TEM Investigations of Biogenic Magnetite Extracted from the Human Hippocampus." *Biochimica et Biophysica Acta,* 1426, 1, 212-216.

Schwickert, F. and Weiss, A. 1972. *Cornerstones of Astrology.* Dallas: Sangreal Foundation.

Seymour, P. 1990. *Astrology: the Evidence of Science.* London: Arkana.

Seymour, P. 2004. *The Scientific Proof of Astrology.* London: Quantum.

Shnoll, S.E. et al. 1998. "Realization of Discrete States During Fluctuations in Macroscopic Processes." *Uspeskhi Fizicheskikh Nauk*, 168 (10), 1129-1140.

Shnoll, S. E. et al. "The specific form of histograms presenting the distribution of data of α-decay measurements appears simultaneously in the moment of New Moon in different points from Artic to Antarctic." http://arxiv.org/ftp/physics/papers/0412/0412152.pdf

Shnoll, S. E. and Panchelyuga, V. A. "Cosmo-physical Effects in the Time Series of the GCP Network." http://arxiv.org/ftp/physics/papers/0605/0605064.pdf

Shnoll, S. E. and Panchelyuga, V. A. "On the Characteristic Form of Histograms Appearing at the Culmination of Solar Eclipse." http://arxiv.org/ftp/physics/papers/0603/0603029.pdf

Silverman, B.I. 1971. "Studies of Astrology." *The Journal of Psychology*, 77, 141-149.

Silverman, B. I. and Whitmer, M. 1974. "Astrological Indicators of Personality." *The Journal of Psychology*, 87, 89-95.

Smit, R. H. "Astrology: My Passion, My Life, My Personal Disaster." http://www.rudolfhsmit.nl/a-pass2.htm)

Smithers, A. G. and Cooper, H. J. 1978. "Personality and Season of Birth." *The Journal of Social Psychology*, 105, 237-241.

Snyder, C.R. 1974. "Why Horoscopes Are True: The Effects of Specificity on Acceptance of Astrological Interpretations." *Journal of Clinical Psychology*, 30, 577-580.

Stacy, D. CSICOP Scare!" http://www.anomalist.com/commentaries/csicop.html

Stelmack, R. M. and Stalikas, A. 1991. "The Humour Theory of Temperament." *Personality and Individual Differences*, vol. 12, 3, 255-263.

Sternberg, R. J. 2000. *Psicologia Cognitiva*. Porto Alegre: Artmed.

Stjernfelt, F. 2001. "A Natural Symphony? To What Extent is Uexküll's Bedeutungslehre Actual for the Semiotics of Our Time?" *Semiotica*, 134, 1/4 , 79-102.

Sugiura, M. et al. 2000. "Correlation Between Human Personality and Neural Activity in Cerebral Cortex." *NeuroImage*, 11, 541-546.

Szekely, A. et al. 2004. Human Personality Dimensions of Persistence and Harm Avoidance Associated with DRD4 and 5-HTTLPR Polymorphisms." *American Journal of Medical Genetics Part B: Neuropsychiatric Genetics*,126B (1), 106-110.

Tavares de Souza, A. 1996. *Curso de História da Medicina: Das Origens ao Fim do Século XVI*. Lisboa: Calouste Gulbenkian.

Thagard. P. K. 1998. "Why Astrology Is a Pseudoscience." (In Klemke, E.D., Hollinger, R. and Wyss, D.: *Introductory Readings in the Philosophy of Science*. New York: Prometheus Books.

Truzzi, M. 1987. "On Pseudo-Skepticism." *Zetetic Scholar*, 12/13, 3-4.

Tyl, N. 1978. *Astrology and Personality*. Saint Paul: Llewellyn.

Tyson, G. A. 1977. "Astrology or Season of Birth: A Split-sphere Test." *The Journal of Psychology*, 95, 285-287.

Uexküll, J. von. 2001. "An Introduction to Umwelt." *Semiotica*, 134, 1/4, 107-110. Original text from 1936.

Urban-Lurain, M. 1981. *Astrology as Science: A Statistical Approach*. Tempe: AFA.

Van Gestel, S. and Van Broeckhoven, C. 2003. Genetics of Personality: Are We Making Progress?" *Molecular Psychiatry*, 8, 840-852.

Veno, A. and Pamment, P. 1979 "Astrology Factors and Personality: A Southern hemisphere Replication." *The Journal of Psychology*, 101, 73-77.

Vernant, J. P. 2002. *As Origens do Pensamento Grego*. Rio de Janeiro: Difel.

Vezzoli, G.C. 2008. "On the Explanation of the Physical Cause of the Shnoll Characteristic Histograms and Observed Fluctuations." *Progress in Physics*, 2, 158-161.

Voet, D. and Voet, J. G. 2006. *Bioquímica*. Porto Alegre: Artmed.

Wade, N. 1977. "A Pyrrhonian Sledgehammer." *Science*, 197, 646.

West, J. A. 1992. *Em Defesa da Astrologia*. São Paulo: Siciliano.

Whittle, S. et al. 2005. "The Neurobiological Basis of Temperament: Towards a Better Understanding of Psychopathology. *Neuroscience and Biobehavioral Reviews*, 30, 511-525.

Wiggins, J. S. 1979. "A Psychological Taxonomy of Trait-descriptive Terms: the Interpersonal Domain." *Journal of Personality and Social Psychology*, 37(3), 395-412.

Wiggins, J. S. 1996. "An informal history of the interpersonal circumplex tradition." *Journal of Personality Assessment*, 66(2) 217-233.

Winklhofer, W. 2005. "Biogenic Magnetite and Magnetic Sensitivity in Organisms—from Magnetic Bacteria to Pigeons." The 15th Riga and 6th PAMIR Conference on Fundamental and Applied MHD.

Wood, J. N. 2003. "Social Cognition and the Prefrontal Cortex." *Behavioral and Cognitive Neuroscience Reviews*, 2(2), 97-114.

Wood, J. N. and Grafman, J. 2003. "Human Prefrontal Cortex: Processing and Representational Perspectives." *Nature Reviews, Neuroscience*, 4, 139-147.

Wright, L. 1997. *Twins and What They Tell Us About Who We Are*. New York: John Wiley & Sons.

Wu, W. 2001. Debunking Common Skeptical Arguments Against Paranormal and Psychic Phenomena. http://www.freeinquiry.com/skeptic/resources/articles/wu-debunking-skeptical)

Wunder, E. 2003. "Self-attribution, Sun-sign Traits, and the Alleged Role of Favourableness as a Moderator Variable: Long-term Effect or Artefact?" *Personality and Individual Differences*, 35(8), 1783-1789.

Youn, T. 2002. "Relationship Between Personality Trait and Regional Cerebral Glucose Metabolism Assesed with Positron Emission Tomography." *Biological Psychology*, 60, 109-120.

Zak, P. J. et al. 2005. "Oxytocin is Associated with Human Trustworthiness." *Hormones and Behavior*, 48, 522-527.

Zak, P. J., et al. 2007. "Oxytocin Increases Generosity in Humans." *PloS ONE*, 2 (11): e1128. http://www.plosone.org/article/info:doi/10.1371/journal.pone.0001128

Zak, P. J. 2008. "A Neurobiologia da Confiança." *Scientific American Brasil*, 6 (74), 64-69.

Zelen, M. 1976. "Astrology and Statistics: A Challenge." *The Humanist*, 36 (1), 32-33.

Zelen, M., Kurtz, P. and Abell, G. 1977. "Is There a Mars Effect?" *The Humanist*, 37 (6), 36-39.

www.ingramcontent.com/pod-product-compliance
Lightning Source LLC
Chambersburg PA
CBHW081849170426
43199CB00018B/2855